T0329171

Cambridge Elements

Austrian Economics
edited by
Peter Boettke
George Mason University

AUSTRIAN CAPITAL THEORY

A Modern Survey of the Essentials

Peter Lewin
University of Texas at Dallas

Nicolas Cachanosky
Metropolitan State University of Denver

CAMBRIDGE
UNIVERSITY PRESS

CAMBRIDGE
UNIVERSITY PRESS

University Printing House, Cambridge CB2 8BS, United Kingdom

One Liberty Plaza, 20th Floor, New York, NY 10006, USA

477 Williamstown Road, Port Melbourne, VIC 3207, Australia

314–321, 3rd Floor, Plot 3, Splendor Forum, Jasola District Centre, New Delhi – 110025, India

79 Anson Road, #06–04/06, Singapore 079906

Cambridge University Press is part of the University of Cambridge.

It furthers the University's mission by disseminating knowledge in the pursuit of education, learning, and research at the highest international levels of excellence.

www.cambridge.org
Information on this title: www.cambridge.org/9781108735889
DOI: 10.1017/9781108696012

© Peter Lewin and Nicolas Cachanosky 2019

First published 2019

A catalogue record for this publication is available from the British Library.

ISBN 978-1-108-73588-9 Paperback
ISSN 2399-651X (online)
ISSN 2514-3867 (print)

Austrian Capital Theory

A Modern Survey of the Essentials

Elements in Austrian Economics

DOI: 10.1017/9781108696012
First published online: January 2019

Peter Lewin
University of Texas at Dallas

Nicolas Cachanosky
Metropolitan State University of Denver

Abstract: In this Element we present a new framework for Austrian capital theory, one that starts from the notion that capital is value. It is the value attributed by the valuer at any moment in time to the combination of production goods and labor available for production. Capital is thus the result obtained by *calculating* the current value of a business unit or business project that employs resources over time. It is the result of a (subjective) entrepreneurial calculation process that relates the value of the *flow* of consumption goods (income, revenue) to the value of the *stocks* of productive resources that will produce those consumptions goods. The entrepreneur is a ubiquitous calculating presence. In a review of the development of Austrian capital theory, by Carl Menger, Eugen von Böhm-Bawerk, Ludwig von Mises, Friedrich Hayek, and Ludwig Lachmann, as well as recent contributions, we endeavor to incorporate the seminal contributions into the new framework in order to provide a more accessible perspective on Austrian capital theory.

Keywords: capital, structure, stocks, flows, discounting, capital heterogeneity, calculation, duration, business cycle, Austrian School

JEL classifications: B1,B2, B13, B25, B53, G1

ISBNs: 9781108735889 (PB), 9781108696012 (OC)
ISSNs: 2399-651X (online), 2514-3867 (print)

Contents

1 Introduction and Background

Austrian capital theory (ACT) suffers from its reputation. Among both scholars of Austrian economics and others who know about it, it is often considered to be an impenetrably complex subject. This is unfortunate. While it is true that the *capital structure* of a modern economy is, indeed, very complex, the *capital theory* that enables us to understand it in terms of the human actions that created it is not. ACT consists of a number of basic elements that, once carefully explained and connected, provide an accessible and very useful account of this theory. To provide such an explanation is the purpose of this Element. We aim to remove any impediment facing the interested scholar seeking to understand the elements of ACT or, indeed, of capital theory more generally.

The reason for ACT's unfavorable reputation lies in its historical development. One might say that the development of ACT suffered a series of unfortunate events. What has come down to us is an account in which the simple basic, commonsense elements of the phenomenon we call "capital" have been obscured as a result of the arcane discussions in its history. Our first order of business, therefore, is to outline these basic elements before turning to the historical development of ACT by examining the work of the theorists who introduced them.

1.1 What Is Capital?

To that end, in this work, for reasons that will become apparent, we promote the commonsense idea of "capital as money," such as when someone says, "This is the capital I can put up to start this business." This way of thinking about capital, as the origin of its name implies,[1] is the conception responsible for the introduction of the word into the language of business and economics.

Somewhere along the line, maybe with Adam Smith's work (1776; see Hodgson, 2014), the concept was broadened to include *physical items*, tools of production. In fact, economists today, when referring to capital, almost always mean the *physical means of production* – sometimes including land, but often excluding it and considering only the *produced* means of production, in other words, tools of production that have been produced by people and not simply inherited "from nature."[2] As a result of this development the relationship between capital as physical productive resources and their *value* in various

---

[1] From medieval Latin, signifying "head," used colloquially to imply "the start of" or "the top of."

[2] Indeed, this issue of whether or not to include natural resources in the definition of capital is just one that complicated the discussions in capital theory. There are important economic differences between resources produced by humans that require maintenance to remain productive and resources simply existing in nature on a permanent basis. And these differences will affect the decisions of the entrepreneur/investor in important ways.

contexts became obscured. A perusal of the literature reveals a frustrating ambiguity in the way that economists speak about capital, sometimes meaning physical equipment, sometimes meaning the financial value of that equipment or of the business as a whole, and often shifting from one to the other without warning. We will show why it is important to be clear about the distinct phenomena at play here, physical and financial.

We shall use an understanding of capital consistent with the following definition by Ludwig von Mises. See Section 7.2.

> Capital is the sum of the *money equivalent* of all assets minus the sum of the *money equivalent* of all liabilities as dedicated at a definite date to the conduct of the operations of a definite business unit. It does not matter in what these assets may consist, whether they are pieces of land, buildings, equipment, tools, goods of any kind and order, claims, receivables, cash, or whatever. (Mises, 1949: 262, italics added; see also Braun et al., 2016 and Braun, 2017)

This definition is remarkably straightforward. Capital is understood as the money value of the "business unit" accounting for all assets and liabilities.[3] Productive activities employ *stocks* of durable and nondurable productive resources over time to produce a *flow* of valuable products or services for use or for sale and, importantly, the value of any combination of productive resources for these purposes depend exclusively on the value of the final goods or services they produce. In fact, there is no defensible way to think about the magnitude of capital except in terms of the flow of income over time that it represents. To attempt to characterize capital in the absence of the income flow that it represents is incoherent. Capital is the conceptual (accounting) tool that relates the value of the flow of final services to the ongoing business that produces them. Capital is the conceptual way to *calculate* (estimate) the value of that business, using finance and accounting conventions.

The value of any business is its *capital value*. Capital is not a physical phenomenon but rather a conceptual one, and as such is *subjective*. It is the result of subjective evaluation. Different evaluators will have different evaluations depending on their expectations relating to the use of the business's productive resources. Only in a comprehensive equilibrium, in which everyone's expectations are identical and correct, will capital values take on any kind of objective characteristics. And, indeed, we all know that a business evaluated

---

[3] The "business unit" can be understood as a shorthand for whatever combination of productive resources is being considered, be it a for-profit business, a nonprofit business, a business division, or even a household, whose productive resources include things like houses, household appliances, raw materials for the production of meals, etc. that are used to produce a stream of valuable services (shelter, comfort, nutrition, etc.) for the owner.

by different appraisers and entrepreneurs will have different values depending on the assumptions made by the appraisers.

It should be obvious that capital can exist only in economic systems that are based on private ownership of resources in which resources and final goods and services can be traded for money. Without private property and markets there would be no way to value productive activity. In short, capital presupposes private property, trade, and money prices. Karl Marx accordingly labeled such a system *capital*ist. In a capitalist system resources tend to move to their highest (capital) value uses. Without private property there is no way to know what the value of alternative uses is. In a socialist system of collective ownership of all resources, with comprehensive central planning, there could be productive resources, but there would be no capital. By understanding the calculative function of capital one can better understand the term "capitalism."

1.2 Financial versus Physical Capital

As mentioned earlier, the meaning of capital in history shifted from the one we have discussed in the foregoing to one connoting the set of physical production goods, or *capital goods*, as they came to be called. Until recently, this was the common conception of the nature of capital in ACT. For example, Eugen von Böhm-Bawerk, the most well-known Austrian capital theorist of his time, focused considerable attention on how to calibrate the "amount of time" taken by any production process, accounting for the production of production goods, while F. A. Hayek and Ludwig Lachmann in different ways concentrated on decisions relating to the *composition* of the produced means of production (production goods[4]) assembled by the producer/entrepreneur. It is not that they ignored the value dimension of capital. Rather, value appears somewhat "in the background" as it were.

A helpful way to think of this is in terms of capital having three different but inseparable "dimensions": value, quantity, and time.[5] There are physical

---

[4] It is important to note that in this Element we use the terms "production goods" and "capital goods" interchangeably.

[5] Strictly speaking there are only two "compound dimensions," quantity and value, both occurring together *in time*. There is *value time* and *quantity time*, and whereas prior work has concentrated markedly the latter, we here promote the former as being the most logical and helpful way to think about the role of time in production and investment (employment) decisions, which is discussed in further detail in the text that follows. Mathematically, this means we are always dealing not so much with magnitudes of single-valued variables such as outputs of q, produced by inputs of l, valued at price p, as with functions of vectors (or time functions), where the stream of outputs q_t valued at prices p_t is produced by a flow of services l_t, etc. This is something with which Hayek (1934, 1941) grappled in trying diagrammatically to portray the dimensions involved.

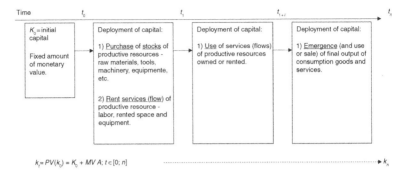

The deployment of capital over time involves the use of productive resources. The initial value of capital (k_0) is augmented.

Figure 1 The deployment of capital over time.

quantities of heterogeneous production goods that are combined over time by the producer to produce valuable outputs. These "capital combinations" thus have a value, derivable from the value of the outputs they produce. This is the relationship between the physical components of any production process and the capital (financial)value of that process. We shall explore this in some detail.

The foregoing discussion has focused on the elusive question of *what* capital is. Capital theory, however, is also concerned with *how* capital is used or applied in the production process. We may imagine the "deployment" of capital to occur in a fashion depicted in Figure 1.

From an initial amount of seed money, K_0 capital is deployed over time to create economic value. The initial investment is enhanced (if the venture is successful) by the the market value added (MVA, the present value of all future economic value added [EVA] in each period). This happens as a result of the transformation of resource service flows into valuable consumption goods and services. Productive resources consist of *stocks* of labor and production goods of many kinds (heterogeneous labor and production goods). Production goods can be owned or rented (their *services* purchased). Labor can be rented for its services, the purchase of which constitutes the flow of wages, but cannot be owned (Rothbard, 2009 [1962]: 488–495). At any moment in time from t_0 to t_n the capital value of the production process (the business venture), k_t, can be derived from the estimated future value of the flow of valuable consumption goods over the life of the business – it is the discounted value of this flow, and will differ from the initial outlay K_0 by the MVA over the production period.

We will expand on this in some detail in Section 9. But first, in Sections 2 through 8, we provide an account of some of the important aspects of the history of the ATC. We do this not merely as an exercise in the history of economic thought, but, more importantly, to reveal how the various components that now make up different perspectives of ACT (as developed by different theorists) – easier to understand in their historical context – ultimately fit together in the new framework that we present in Section 9.

2 Carl Menger and the Structure of Production

2.1 Carl Menger: Free Goods and Economics Goods; Consumption Goods and Services and Production Goods and Services; Stocks and Flows

Carl Menger, the founding theorist of the Austrian School of Economics, suggested that the material world was composed of goods and services and considered the end of all economic activity to be the consumption of valuable services produced by goods of various "orders." He divided goods into two exclusive kinds: free goods and economic goods. Free goods are those for which, at a zero price, less would be desired than is available. By contrast, economic goods are those for which, at a zero price, more would be desired than is available. Economic goods are scarce, have value, and will command a positive price if freely traded. Economic goods have value because they yield desirable services. These services provide consumers with utility.

Economic goods may, in turn, be divided into two types: those whose services yield utility directly, first order or consumption goods, and those whose services provide utility indirectly, production goods, or higher-order goods. Production goods provide services that are used in the production of other production goods successively in a supply chain leading to the emergence of consumer goods that provide services yielding utility. Thus, the value of all goods derives ultimately from the utility of the services of consumer goods (Israel Kirzner has called this "Menger's Law").

The distinction between stocks and flows is fundamental and important and often neglected. People do not desire goods "in themselves"; they desire what flows from having or renting them. It is the services of goods that are the ultimate objective of economic action. As Menger points out, these can be obtained directly from nature or indirectly by production, using produced instruments of production, production goods.

2.2 Production Takes Time

Menger talks of higher-order goods being sequentially "transformed" until their emergence as consumption goods. At an early stage in the development of civilization people learn that they can do more than simply "gather the goods of lowest order that happen to be offered by nature" (1871: 75) and can deliberately and carefully fashion more productive means of production, production goods. Doing so, however, takes time.

> The transformation of goods of higher order into goods of lower order takes place, as does every other process of change, in time. The times at which men will obtain command of goods of first order from the goods of higher order in their present possession will be more distant the higher the order of these goods. (Menger, 1871: 152)

Production goods thus exist at any moment in time in a *structure of production*. The structure of production reflects the fact that production takes time. Some production services must be used sooner than others, and some production services must be used together as complementary inputs. Because production takes time, and because time is valuable, the "longer" the process of production the more productive of utility it must be in order to be economically justifiable. And the longer one takes in production, the more opportunity is available to perfect the quality and/or increase the quantity of what is being produced.

> [B]y making progress in the employment of goods of higher orders for the satisfaction of their needs, economizing men can most assuredly increase the consumption goods available to them accordingly—but *only on condition that they lengthen the periods of time over which their activity is to extend* in the same degree that they progress to goods of higher order. (Menger, 1976: 153, italics added)

Economic development is characterized by an increasing "lengthening" of production processes. We see this as the increasing accumulation of sophisticated production goods (machines) and production processes. Thus, economic development has been accompanied by the improvement of production technology over time. People have learned to do things better by using increasingly specialized production goods. At any point in time, however, the knowledge that men have of the value of their production projects will be less than complete. As production occurs in time, and as the passage of time necessarily implies the existence of uncertainty, investors/entrepreneurs will be uncertain as to both the viability of certain kinds of production processes and their economic value in terms of the utility they will ultimately yield. Error is inevitable and is a necessary part of the learning process.

As Adam Smith realized, the degree of specialization in production depends crucially on the size of the market for the final product. The size of the market is measured by the number of units of product that can be sold. Menger realized that the size of markets, given by the number of the transactions they facilitate, depends crucially on the use of a medium of exchange. He explained how goods of high marketability have evolved into money (Menger, 1871, 1892).

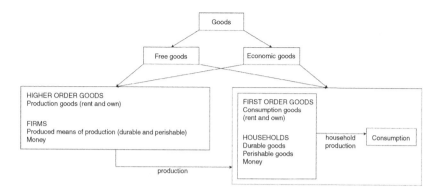

Figure 2 Menger's world of goods and services.

The use of money multiplies exchange and specialized production. And money, as a unit of exchange value in all market exchanges, serves also to *measure* the value of production and exchange. In any exchange the money price of the good or service being exchanged is a reflection of the utility to both the buyer and the seller. In fact, as money facilitates production and exchange we may regard it as a higher-order good in the service of producing consumer utility. It is, however, a rather special kind of higher-order good, as it is traded in all markets (see Figure 2).

Menger affirms the crucial distinction between stocks of useful goods and the flow of their services. The object of human action is not the goods themselves but rather the services they yield, directly (consumption goods) or indirectly (production goods). It may actually be more sensible to regard all goods, which may be durable (such as machinery and household appliance) or perishable (such as raw materials and food items), as types of production goods producing, directly or indirectly, consumption services. Production goods thus exist both in firms and in households. For example, the purchase of a house, which is a durable asset, is the purchase of a good that produces consumption services (residence, shelter, etc.) over a long period of time. (See Figure 2 .)

2.3 Menger's View of Capital Is Implied by His View of Subjective Value

This theory of capital in Menger's founding work is completely consistent with his seminal contribution to the subjective theory of value that was a paradigm shift in economics, completely transforming the discipline from one focused on the study of wealth, perceived to be objective (plutology), to one based on exchange (catallactics) (Lachmann, 1986: 145).

Classical economics was, at least originally, a pragmatic discipline. Its aim was to study means to increase the "wealth of nations". Its orientation is thus to a macroeconomic magnitude. It needed a measure of wealth, and the classical notion of value was primarily designed to serve this need. Production and distribution of wealth was what really mattered. The consumer was an outsider, not an economic agent . . . . Markets, in classical doctrine, contained producers and merchants only. All this changed when subjective utility replaced objective (and measurable) cost of production as the source of value.

Economics now had to find a place for the consumer. It was he, after all, who now bestowed value on objects. All non-consumer goods were now shown to have at best purely derivative value. . . . each consumer as an individual would now assign value to objects which become economic goods as a result of his action. (Lachmann, 1986: 145)

The ACT is nothing less than the *subjective* theory of capital value. All value emanates from the preferences of individual consumers acting and interacting on the basis of those preferences. Menger realized that trading prices represented the *marginal value* to each trading partner. It represents a value at least as high as the best alternative the buyer could have purchased with the money price, and to the seller the money price represents the value of something he can purchase that is at least as great as what he has given up. And on this basis a whole new economics was forged. Consumers value the services flowing from stocks of consumer goods. Thus, those stocks, and the stocks of producer goods used to create them, have value only because consumers value those consumption flows.

3 Böhm-Bawerk's Labor Arithmetic

Menger's disciple Eugen von Böhm-Bawerk produced a voluminous work elaborating, as he saw it, Menger's original vision on capital. However, in the process of this elaboration, Böhm-Bawerk strayed from the subjectivism of Menger's vision.

3.1 Böhm-Bawerk and the Productivity of Roundabout Production

Böhm-Bawerk (1890) picked up on Menger's insight that time plays a crucial role in production and in economic growth and development. As economic growth and rising incomes allow producers to take more time in the development of better and more efficient production techniques, production becomes more "roundabout," more complex. Roundabout methods of production will be chosen only if they are more productive of value (utility). Complex production goods and techniques (and the same might be said of labor services) are developed.

This can sometimes be confusing. Looking at production in a modern economy at any point in time, it is true that the production of most things is done more "quickly" in the sense that, *once specialized equipment is in place,* it takes *less time* to produce anything. Time is saved by having the right tools. But this is true only because, in another sense, *more time* was taken at some point in the past to produce those specialized tools. It is in this latter sense that Böhm-Bawerk considers roundabout production to be more time-consuming. The setting up of complex production equipment and networks requires savings (abstaining from consumption) and time. But once in place, the reward is quicker, more reliable production processes. The division of labor, essentially a division of function and knowledge, is an organizing principle (in large part spontaneous), which has resulted in massive increases in the volume and variety of useful consumption goods produced.

Böhm-Bawerk considered more "roundabout" production methods to be, *ceteris paribus,* more productive of output, but also imagined that as the length of production was extended, increases in productivity would be subject to diminishing returns (presumably as long as technology remains unchanged).

3.2 Böhm-Bawerk and the Problem of Measuring the Average Period of Production

In referring to roundabout production, Böhm-Bawerk wanted to highlight the role of time, namely the intuition that complex, specialized production pro-cesses have come to embody "more" time. Requiring more time is an important aspect of a project that the potential investor must take into account in apprais-ing it. If one has to wait longer on average for its rewards, one must be compensated for the wait. But what exactly does it mean to say "wait longer"? It was this that Böhm-Bawerk sought to answer with his construction of the average period of production, the APP.

Böhm-Bawerk tried to find a measure of the amount of time embodied in any project, looked at from any perspective, in the sense of how much time it would take to set up that project from scratch (tracing the components all the way back to the original nature-given substances and labor it would hypothetically take to build everything that is needed). In pushing this line of reasoning, the more precise he endeavored to become, the more ambiguous and elusive his essential point became. We may explain this briefly as follows.

Realizing that some arbitrariness attached to the period over which any productive combination extends, from the original labor (and land) to the final product – having to contemplate points far back in time – Böhm-Bawerk proposed a more tractable measure of time that he called the *average period of production* (APP). The APP is the labor-weighted average of the amount of time applied in the project. It is an input-weighted average. It relies on the ability to add up units of labor – that is, it presumes that labor services are homogeneous and can be used to gauge the intensity of time applied (labor hours).

Böhm-Bawerk considers only labor, ignoring the contribution of the "original" resources of land (nature), which he considered to be an innocuous simplification in the modern world. He wanted to capture the idea that production processes that use produced means of production, such as machines and raw materials, take a great deal of time if one considers the time and effort necessary to produce not only the final product with their help, but also to produce those produced means of production themselves as well. He wanted to conceptually reduce all produced means of production to their original labor inputs and then to add up the amount of labor time involved and to use the measure of labor time to weight the significance of the time involved in production.

By way of explanation we provide an example in Table 1 (see Böhm-Bawerk, 1890: 87). Table 1 depicts a production process that takes 10 periods from the start to the finish (at which point the final product emerges). The period number is tabulated in column 1. In each period labor is applied to the unfinished product. The labor applied in any period, l_t, (column 2) is "embodied" in the production process for a period of time equal to the number of periods remaining in the production process, $n - t$ (column 3). Column 4 contains the weighted labor input for each period, calculated as the product of columns 2 and 3, divided by the total (unweighted) amount of labor input, 90 units, the total of column 2. The total of this column (column 4) is the APP (6.39 periods). If we use the symbols at the top of the columns, the formula for the APP is as in equation 1,

$$\text{APP} = \sum_{t=1}^{n} \left\{ \underbrace{\frac{l_t}{\sum_{t=1}^{n} l_t}}_{\text{weight}} * \underbrace{(n - t)}_{\text{time}} \right\} \tag{1}$$

This has a straightforward interpretation. Each time period, $n - t$ (amount of time), involved is weighted by the relative amount of labor applied in that period, and added up. The APP is the total amount of time measured by the amount of time in production, adding up the periods, weighted by the relative

Table 1 Calculating Böhm-Bawerk's average period of production

1	2	3	4
	Number of labor	**Production**	
Period no.	**hours applied**	**period**	**Weighted input**
			$\frac{l_t}{\sum_{t=1}^{n} l_t} * (n - t)$
t	l_t	$n - t$	
1	5	10	0.56
2	10	9	1.00
3	20	8	1.78
4	15	7	1.17
5	10	6	0.67
6	10	5	0.56
7	8	4	0.36
8	6	3	0.20
9	4	2	0.09
10	2	1	0.02
n	$90 = \sum_{t=1}^{n} l_t$	55	$6.39 = \sum_{t=1}^{n} \left\{ \frac{l_t}{\sum_{t=1}^{n} l_t} * (n - t) \right\}$

amount of labor applied in that period. In this way one arrives at an "average" amount of time, or an *average period of production*.

3.3 But What Does It Mean?

Böhm-Bawerk plausibly did not consider it possible as a practical matter to actually measure the APP in many or any instances. He presumably offers it for illustration of how, in principle, it might be measured, and, in his textual remarks, seems to suggest that in practice it is intuitively clear which processes have a higher or lower APP. He does this by way of numerous examples of production processes (see Böhm-Bawerk, 1890: 79–118).

But if the construction of the APP strikes you as mechanical with an obscure connection to economics, it is because it is. It is really only a small part of Böhm-Bawerk's work on the role of time in production, but one that garnered considerable attention, much of it negative. It behooves us therefore to examine it a bit more closely to tease out the intuition Böhm-Bawerk was chasing and the problems he inadvertently invited in the process.

Having asserted that time was important and that the "more time" a production process took, the more productive it could be expected to be, he was challenged to explain precisely what he meant by "more time." Is 2 units of labor applied for 3 periods more or less than 3 units of labor applied for 2 periods? To solve this he decided to consider hours of labor adjusted for the number of laborers – labor hours. Next, it did not make sense to consider the total number of periods for which labor was applied. To be meaningful, a measure of the "time taken" in production had to account for each period in terms of its *relative* significance in the production process as a whole. The most obvious way to measure that relative significance is in terms of the relative amount (proportion) of the total amount of labor hours applied. In the example in Table 1, note that a proportionally higher amount of labor is applied in the early periods than in the later periods, giving them more weight and pushing the average above the simple midpoint of the production period. In a later application by Friedrich Hayek, as we shall see in Section 4, matters are arranged so that the APP is indeed simply one-half of the total production period – a result that would be expected if all the weights were equal or earlier ones just balance out later ones.

One question immediately suggests itself. What exactly is the role of time in production? Why do equal amounts of labor hours applied earlier in the production process carry more weight than those applied later in the process? Böhm-Bawerk provides no answer to this. In fact, the mystery is the source of a fundamental contradiction in the APP. Böhm-Bawerk was seeking a measure of time that could be used to illustrate the positive connection between "time taken" and value produced. As such he wanted that measure to be a purely physical one, not a value one. It should contain no presumption of value added if it is to be an independent *explanation* of value added. But clearly, the construction of the APP invites the interpretation that value must be added in each period if the production process is to be justified, enough value so that the extra time taken is justified. Such an interpretation would have to have the value added in each period at least equal to the "cost of time" for that period. This "cost of time" is what is captured in interest rates.

This interpretation would imply that, contrary to appearances and to Böhm-Bawerk's intention, the APP is a *value* construct. Böhm-Bawerk was aware of this problem and tried to avoid it by assuming that value was added according to simple interest, not compound interest. Using only simple interest, it can be shown that the implied interest rate appears in the numerator and the denominator of the APP formula in a way that it cancels out. The APP thus remains independent of value, and specifically independent of the magnitude of interest assumed to be applied in each (calendar[6]) period (see the mathematical note in

---

[6] In fact, there are two distinct conceptions of time used in the APP. One is the amount of "labor time" applied at any point of time in the production process. Böhm-Bawerk found himself

the text that follows). But clearly, this is an ad hoc, indefensible move. It is compound accumulation (interest) that is required for the construct to make economic sense, and, if compound interest is included, the APP becomes a value construct that depends on the rate of interest and cannot be used to explain it or the enhanced productivity of roundaboutness (see the Mathematical Note that follows below).

As we shall see, whenever time is involved, value necessarily enters into the calculation in the form of the rate of discount (or accumulation). Inputs applied at different points in time do not exchange one for one. In that way the APP came to be seen as problematic – and in other ways too[7] (Lewin, 2011,: 69–78).

Mathematical Note: APP, Simple and Compound Interest

If simple interest at the rate of r per period augments the value of labor invested in the product, the APP formula can be written

$$\text{APP} = \tau = \sum_{t=1}^{n} \left\{ \frac{l_t \left(1+(n-t)r\right)}{\sum_{t=1}^{n} l_t \left(1+(n-t)r\right)} * (n-t) \right\}$$

We can use τ as follows to calculate the *total interest paid* on the accumulated inputs:

$$\sum_{t=1}^{n} l_t \left(1 + (n-t)r\right) = \left(\sum_{t=1}^{n} l_t\right) * (1 + \tau r)$$

Now solving for τ, we can show that it does not depend on r.

"backed into" this "time as factor of production" conception by his desire to adjust for the "amount of time taken" over the life of the production process. Hayek later repeated this move. The second is the notion of *calendar* time, time in the sense of the "passing of time" as we experience it. The two concepts are, for example, conflated in the "aging wine" example of a production process. The passage of time itself appears productive, because something physical happens automatically as time passes that makes the wine more valuable as a product. These two distinct conceptions are related to the ubiquitous confusing relationship between the quantity and value dimensions of capital mentioned earlier.

[7] Other problems discussed by Böhm-Bawerk's critics (most notably J. B. Clark, 1888, 1893) included the question of how to decide when a project begins and ends. Other problems include the assumption that all labor is homogeneous and can be simply aggregated, the neglect of the inputs of land, ambiguity about whether the output is a physical quantity or a value (Böhm-Bawerk considers the production of a single homogeneous product and never talks about how this may be extended to a multiproduct or a multiprocess situation), and ambiguity about and neglect of the question of the connection between capital accumulation and technological change. All in all, as we shall show, the APP is both problematic and unnecessary for an understanding of capital.

$$\left(\sum_{t=1}^{n} l_t\right) + \left(\sum_{t=1}^{n} l_t(n-t)r\right) = \left(\sum_{t=1}^{n} l_t\right) * (1 + \tau r)$$

r cancels out of both sides of the equation and

$$\tau = \sum_{t=1}^{n} \left\{ \frac{l_t}{\sum_{t=1}^{n} l_t} * (n-t) \right\} \text{ as in equation 1}$$

This reveals the APP as equivalently a value construct, with value measured by labor hours. So, ironically, Böhm-Bawerk can be seen to have arrived (inadvertently) at a Ricardian "labor theory of value" construct.

If, instead, the inputs are seen to grow at a compound rate, then r will not cancel out in the expression,

$$\tau = \sum_{t=1}^{n} \left\{ \frac{l_t(1+r)^{(n-t)}}{\sum_{t-1}^{n} l_t(1+r)^{(n-t)}} * (n-t) \right\},$$

and the APP looks exactly like a modern financial formula known as *duration* (for an historical process, looking back from the present and calculating present value). It turns out that the only defensible measure of "average time" is one based on accumulating value added, like *duration*, something we shall explain fully in Section 9.6.

3.4 Looking Back and Looking Forward; the Retreat to Ricardian Equilibrium

Table 1 can serve to illustrate two different perspectives. One can consider it to depict an investor's estimate of the amount of labor time that in the future will be involved in a particular investment project. The APP is thus an estimate of the amount of time on average that will be required to take the project to completion. One may shorten the calendar time involved by applying labor more intensively in each period. The APP measures the average time-as-effort needed.

Alternatively, Table 1 can refer to an ongoing project that is continually producing units of a final product by applying labor over 10 periods in the manner described. From this perspective, the APP measures the average amount of time involved looking backward or forward at an unchanging production process, where the required inputs and the expected outputs are known with certainly. Only in a robust systemic equilibrium are the two perspectives equivalent. Böhm-Bawerk shifted from the first forward-looking perspective to the second static equilibrium one.

In other words, Böhm-Bawerk shifted focus from the question of how much time on average it can be said an investor has to anticipate before his investment comes to fruition to the question of how much time can be said to be embodied already in any given (even completed) project. A *prospective* or *forward*-looking perspective morphed into a *retrospective* or *backward*-looking perspective – or into a discussion in which the two are interchangeable. In a changing world, "looking back" is not the same as "looking forward" but in a static equilibrium world (an evenly rotating economy) they are. In such a world, projects look the same at whatever point in time one looks at them. Böhm-Bawerk moved away from Menger's implicitly dynamic view of the world to a static view that had more in common with Ricardo than with Menger (Hicks, 1973a; Lewin, 2011: 102) – an ironic and momentous turn.

Both the shift in perspective and the use of an input-weighted measure departed significantly from the original vision laid out by Menger, which purportedly led Menger to regard Böhm-Bawerk's treatment of capital and time as a serious mistake. An article by Menger published in 1888 on the nature of capital can be read along these lines (Braun, 2015a).[8] In any case, the APP provoked a vigorous response leading to the accumulation of a large literature, the first of the three famous "capital controversies."

Problematic or not, Böhm-Bawerk's approach was very influential and provided a basis for work done by Austrians, neoclassicals, and Marxists (neo-Ricardians). From a Mengerian perspective, it was a wrong turn with far-reaching consequences. It fueled Hayek's approach to the business cycle, the neoclassical development of the production function, and it was involved at some level in all of the three so-called capital controversies. In retrospect, Böhm-Bawerk's was a most "un-Austrian" of moves. His conception of the production process in terms of the quantity of its inputs appears to be a decisive move against subjectivism. Nevertheless, the vast literature in capital and growth theory related directly or indirectly to Böhm-Bawerk's conception did raise some interesting questions from which Austrians learned a great deal, even as they attempted to grapple with what was right and what was wrong with Böhm-Bawerk's approach (Lewin, 2011: 73–78).

The most important "learning experience" in the application of a version of Böhm-Bawerk's capital theory occurred in the 1930s when F. A. Hayek

---

[8] "Menger, … severely condemned Böhm-Bawerk's theory from the first. In his somewhat grandiloquent style he told me once: 'The time will come when people will realize that Böhm-Bawerk's theory is one of the greatest errors ever committed.' He [Schumpeter] deleted those hints in his 2nd edition." (Schumpeter, 1954: 847, note 8). See Bornier (2016).

attempted to marry it to the Austrian theory of the business cycle (ABCT), which is the subject of our next section.

4 Austrian Capital Theory and Austrian Business Cycle Theory

4.1 Hayek's Triangle: A Special Case of Böhm-Bawerk's Special Case

The 1930s was a period of great difficulty for Austrian economics, albeit one of some notable contributions. It was a time of decisive turning away from an appreciation of competitive capitalist economic systems toward socialism; it was a period of ascendancy for formalism in economic discourse at the expense of economic reasoning based on subjective value; it was a period of the emergence of Keynesian economics and its focus on macroaggregates to the exclusion of microeconmic foundations; and it was a period of renewed attack on ACT as inherited from Böhm-Bawerk.

Though all related, the last mentioned difficulty was in part the result of the fact that ambiguity and obscurity surrounding ACT was aggravated by Hayek's use of it in his *Prices and Production* (1931), a work designed to explain the deepening economic downturn that was at the time developing. In that work Hayek lays great emphasis on the structure of production as conceived in Böhm-Bawerk's framework. To explain the process of a credit-induced business cycle (originally developed by Mises [1912]) – what has become known as the Mises–Hayek theory of the business cycle, or the Austrian Business Cycle Theory (ABCT), he borrows from Böhm-Bawerk and constructs his own special case (originally conceived by Jevons [1871], chapter VII) – basically a stylized or simplified version of Böhm-Bawerk's already special case.

As with Böhm-Bawerk, the focus is on the physical aspects of production and time. He considers a special case in which the flow of inputs (exclusively units of homogeneous labor) is constant over time. If the same amount of labor time, l_0, is applied in each period, then, from our foregoing discussion of Böhm-Bawerk's APP, applying equation 1,

$$\sum_{t=1}^{n}(n-t)l_t = \tfrac{1}{2}n(n+1)l_0 \text{ and since } \sum_{t=0}^{n}l_t = nl_0 \text{ the APP} \approx \tfrac{n}{2}^9$$

In other words, very intuitively, the average period of production is equal to half of the total time taken from the first input to the emergence of the final

---

[9] APP $=\tfrac{1}{2}n+\tfrac{1}{2}\approx\tfrac{1}{2}n$ (when n is large enough to ignore the $\tfrac{1}{2}$ or when the APP is expressed in continuous time and therefore is absent).

output. This can be easily illustrated by a variation of our earlier example (Table 1) in Table 2 (see Böhm-Bawerk, 1890: 86).

In this simple case each unit of input is "locked up" on average for (approximately) half the length of the production period.[10] Hayek (1931) uses a triangle to represent the idea of roundaboutness, where the APP is halfway along the base of a triangle, as illustrated in Figure 3. The horizontal axis is a measure of labor time. The assumption is that inputs are applied uniformly over time (column 2). If the inputs were not applied uniformly the graphical simplification would not work. It is the amount of labor hours *and* how long they are "locked up" that constitutes the degree of roundaboutness. With this graphical representation Hayek attempted to capture the vision of Menger, Jevons, and Böhm-Bawerk (and, notably, Wicksell[11]) about the structure of production and to marry it to a vision of the business cycle developed by Ludwig von Mises (1912).

Following Böhm-Bawerk in assuming simple interest, the accumulated value of the labor inputs rises at a constant rate and traces out a straight line above the accumulated inputs. The APP is (approximately) halfway along the time axis – at the midpoint – independent of the rate of interest. But this is no longer true if interest is compounded, in which case the accumulated value rises exponentially and the APP is dependent on the size of the interest rate. l_0 of labor is applied in each of periods 1 through 10. If no interest is applied, the value of the unfinished product accumulates by the amount of l_0 per period. This is the line that accumulates to the total nl_0. If interest is accumulated at a rate of r per period, *simple interest*, then $l_0 r$ is added to the accumulated value in each period, finally reaching a value of $nl_0(1+r)$ in the 10th period. By contrast, if interest is applied at a rate of r in each period, *compound interest*, then the value reached in each period accumulates at a rate of $(1+r)^t$, where t, the time period (the accumulated value up to that point, is multiplied by $(1+r)^t$, finally reaching a value of $l_0(1+r)^n$ in the 10th period.

4.2 Introducing Stages of Production

Hayek's triangle puts together two related concepts, the average period of production and the different *stages of production*. He presents a simple sequential "supply-chain" model where each stage of production sells its output as input to the next stage of production until the consumption stage is reached at the end of the process. Mining, for instance, precedes refining, which in turn

---

[10] See previous footnote.

[11] For a comprehensive overview of Wicksell's various contributions to capital theory see Uhr (1960), chapter V.

Table 2 Calculating Böhm-Bawerk's average period of production: Hayek's special case

1 Period	2 Number of labor hours applied	3 Production period	4 Weighted input
t	l_t	$n - t$	$\dfrac{l_t}{\sum_{t=1}^{n} l_t} * (n - t)$
1	1	10	1.00
2	1	9	0.90
3	1	8	0.80
4	1	7	0.70
5	1	6	0.60
6	1	5	0.50
7	1	4	0.40
8	1	3	0.30
9	1	2	0.20
10	1	1	0.10
n	$10 = \sum_{t=1}^{n} l_t = n l_0$	$55 = \sum_{t=1}^{n}(n - t)$	$5.50 = \sum_{t=1}^{n}\left\{\dfrac{l_t}{\sum_{t=1}^{n} l_t} * (n - t)\right\}$
		$= \tfrac{1}{2} n \cdot (n + 1)$	$= \left(\tfrac{1}{10}\right) * 55$
		$= \tfrac{1}{2} (10 * 11)$	

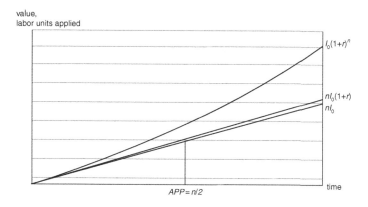

Figure 3 Hayek's triangle: simple and compound interest at 5%.

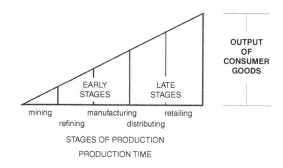

Figure 4 Hayekian triangle and stages of production.
Source: Garrison (2001: 47)

precedes manufacturing, which is followed by distributing and then retailing as the final stage of production before reaching the consumer (see Figure 4, borrowed from Garrison [2001]). The height at the end of each stage shows the value added up to that point in the production process. Note this moving away from Böhm-Bawerk's objective measure of labor to attaching a market value to the concept of period of production (measured vertically in Figure 4).

Hayek's triangle is intuitive and useful as an expository device. It is effective to illustrate the argument that the degree of roundaboutness (i.e., number of stages of production) that can be sustained depends on the time preferences of consumers. A fall in consumers' time preferences at the margin (the reluctance to postpone consumption and increase savings) allows stages of production to be added, thus increasing the accumulated value added at the end of the triangle. In other words, the increase in savings allows a move toward a more "capital-intensive" structure of production with a higher pay-off at the end of the process. By the same token, a fall in the interest rate that is produced by an increase in the supply of money and/or credit, in the absence of an increase in savings provided by consumers, would send a false signal to producers, who might try to add stages of production as a result. But their efforts would, in time, be unstainable, because the necessary resources to sustain these new or expanded ventures are not really available. Consumers have not reduced their demand for output to release resources for production. So the shift, and likely change of slope, of the diagonal of the triangle would be temporary, illustrating the boom of a cycle, while the bust would entail a reversal of the move. This is the essence of the ABCT illustrated by Hayek with this framework.

The simplifications introduced in Hayek's triangle in *Prices and Production*, after some initial accolades, produced a storm of criticism. His model invited confusion and contributed to the rejection of Böhm-Bawerk's capital theory (and, with it, the distinctive aspect of the ABCT). The fact that a stage of production is an abstract tool (used to study capital theory) rather than an observable objective reality[12] adds doubts about Böhm-Bawerk's roundabout-ness story. The same observed reality can be represented by different stages of production (which can be more or less than the five represented). To define a Hayekian triangle requires a set of subjective assumptions about how to identify separate stages of production given the available data. In the first place, one (or more) economic activities can be present in different stages. For instance, the supply of energy or financial services is present along the whole production process. What should be the relative position of industries like these two? Second, there is the phenomenon of "looping," the situation in which two different industries supply inputs to each other. The energy market supplies electricity to banks, which in turn provide financial services to the energy sector. Which industry should precede the other as a stage of produc-tion? Third, it is possible that an industry identified as being at a particular stage of production may change its relative position over the course of a business cycle.[13] Fourth, Luther and Cohen (2014) argue that a stage of production can grow not only vertically (increase in value added) but also horizontally, and this can significantly affect how the effects on the structure of production are interpreted if vertical changes are the only modification assumed to take

---

[12] This is very clear from Hayek's later and final comprehensive work on capital theory (1941a) in which he routinely refers to stages by enclosing the word in quotes, as in "stages" (Hayek, 1941a: 131–132, 140–142, 146–147).

[13] Young (2012) offers evidence of this problem for the USA between 2002 and 2007.

place. The simplicity embedded in Hayek's triangle cannot be translated into the complexity of reality without facing nontrivial challenges.[14]

4.3 The Legacy of Hayek's Triangle

During the 1930s, Hayek had attempted to flesh out the capital theory underlying his approach to business cycles in numerous articles, culminating finally in his book *The Pure Theory of Capital* published in 1941 to take account of the many complications that render his simple triangle problematic. Against the backdrop of World War II and the ascendancy of Keynesian economics, Hayek sought to solidify his contention that inappropriately low central-bank-induced interest rates distorted the structure of production, and that the unemployment that ensued was a result of the unsustainable structure of heterogeneous capital goods that had been constructed. As Keynes had pointed out, in a monetary economy individual acts of saving and individual acts of investment are separate and may be inconsistent. Keynes and Hayek disagreed about the implications of this. For Keynes this was a reason to doubt the stability of financial markets and the capacity of the economy to self-correct.

Hayek's triangle was a response to this. But the triangle was his medium, not his message. He chose the triangle as a simple way to communicate the message, which actually required a much deeper and more detailed understanding of capital theory to be fully appreciated. What was the essence of this message?

For Hayek, as with the classical economists, interest rate movements were necessary and sufficient to coordinate the plans of savers and investors. This coordination, however, was disrupted if the central bank engaged in credit expansion to reduce interest rates. As Hayek saw it, the implications of this are that credit-induced (as distinct from savings-induced) low interest rates provided a false signal that caused discoordination between savers and investors; specifically, the low interest rates provided an incentive for reduced saving and increased investment, with the gap being closed by an elastic money supply. Given the fall in saving, or by implication the increase in consumption, the amount of investment is insufficient to supply current consumption demands.

---

[14] The inspiration for much of contemporary empirical research on the ABCT is Garrison's (2001) use of Hayek's triangle. This line of work investigates whether different industries (stages of production) behave as predicted by Garrison's model representation of the ABCT, where it is expected that early and later stages of production grow (vertically) with respect to mid-stages of production (Lester & Wolff, 2013; Luther & Cohen, 2014; Mulligan, 2002; Powell, 2002; Young, 2005). There are, however, a few exceptions (Cachanosky, 2014; Koppl, 2014; Young, 2012). These authors either look at an aggregate average period of production (roundaboutness) for the whole economy or interest rate sensitivity of different industries rather than looking at stages of production.

But it is not so much that investment is insufficient as that it is the *wrong kind* of investment, investment in production projects that are too "long" – too "capital-intensive." This required him to provide a firm understanding of how one determines the "length" any investment project, the investment period, and how this related to the "amount" of capital invested in it, and, furthermore, to show that the lower the interest rate the greater the investment period/capital intensity that would result from the investment decisions of entrepreneurs.

To explain the business cycle by appealing to the nature of capital, it turns out that the heterogeneity of capital goods is necessary. We talk about heterogeneity in Section 6.2, but need to explain here why it is important to ABCT. The heterogeneous nature of capital goods, particularly the fact that they cannot generally be substituted one for the other, but rather have specific and restricted uses and must be assembled in complementary combinations as part of the production process, implies that they cannot simply be reallocated to more sustainable projects once the current project is revealed as unsustainable. Investments in capital combinations are not reversible. (The dimensions of the triangle cannot be easily changed and then changed back.) Once investment in specific capital goods has been made in an unsustainable, unprofitable venture, capital losses will occur and the value of the specific goods involved will be revealed lower than previously thought. This constitutes the depression phase of the cycle. Absent heterogeneity the investments could simply be undone and redone in a more profitable way, without much loss.

In using the ACT, and its particular formulation by Böhm-Bawerk, as the foundation for developing a theory of the business cycle, Hayek thus became committed to a particular framework *that relied on the absence of heterogeneity (or at least suppressed it) to illustrate the consequences of the fact of heterogeneity.* This resulted in the rejection or ignoring of the ABCT over the decades. His later examination of the complexities of capital showed that, even in equilibrium, it was impossible to attach an unambiguous meaning to the concept of "average period of production" or to show that such a quantity was monotonically related to the interest (discount) rate. While he was able to decisively confirm the importance of time for a thorough understanding of production decisions, and while he was able, under some restrictive assumptions, to give clear meaning to the notion of the multiple investment periods involved in any ongoing investment project – connecting inputs to outputs over time – he was forced to abandon the attempt to characterize investment projects in the form of a single magnitude like the APP.

> As at first contemplated, this study was intended as little more than a
> systematic exposition of what I imagined to be a fairly complete body of

doctrine which, in the course of years, had evolved from the foundations laid by Jevons, Böhm-Bawerk and Wicksell. I had little idea . . . that some of the simplifications employed by the earlier writers had such far-reaching consequences as to make their conceptual tools almost useless in the analysis of more complicated situations. The most important of these inappropriate simplifications . . . was the attempt to introduce the time factor into the theory of capital in the form of one single relevant time interval – the "average period of production." (Hayek, 1941a: 3–4; see also 92–93)

The first edition of Hayek's *Prices and Production* was published in 1931 and contained the simplified version of Böhm-Bawerk's approach explained earlier. In 1941 Hayek published *The Pure Theory of Capital*, an attempt to provide a fully worked out response to the critical reactions to the simplified capital theory in *Prices and Production*. But much of the content of *Pure Theory* was completed before its publication because during the intervening decade Hayek had published numerous articles on different aspects of the subject, the substance of which ultimately came to be incorporated in the 1941 book. For various reasons, *Pure Theory* did not achieve its objective "to develop a capital theory that could be fully integrated into business cycle theory" (White, 2007: xxiii – xiv). Rather, to this day, most of those working on ABCT explicitly or implicitly take the *Prices and Production* version (Hayek's simple triangle) as their framework, use the "stages of production" metaphor, and refer to "longer" or "shorter" production processes as though no ambiguity attached to these concepts. In *Pure Theory*, Hayek had hoped to provide a more defensible alternative that dealt sufficiently with these ambiguities. The fact that he was not successful is of interest in comprehending ACT today and its potential to illuminate, among other things, the nature of monetarily induced business cycles.

Where does this leave the ABCT? This is something we shall take up in Section 9 to show that there is an alternative approach to the question of credit-induced malinvestment different from the one offered by Hayek. As stated earlier, Hayek himself attempted to modify capital theory to render it more suitable for an exposition of the business cycle, but largely failed. We examine this briefly in the next section.

5 Hayek's Capital Theory

Like the concept of the APP, a related claim seemed strongly intuitive. The claim was that expanding money and credit in a way that reduced market interest rates could encourage spending on relatively "longer-term" investment projects that were not sustainable, and, that, if this effect were strong enough, it would ultimately produce a correction, showing up statistically as a business cycle. It was a claim that seemed to have its confirmation in various historical episodes if interpreted along those lines. Furthermore, it was a claim that Hayek said he "knew" to be correct but had yet, even after the publication of *Pure Theory*, still to prove.[15]

In his work on capital theory during the 1930s Hayek had tried in various ways to find an alternative to the APP to support what he felt he knew about business cycles. In the process he was led to consider also other aspects of capital theory, for example, the questions of "capital consumption,", capital maintenance, capital accumulation and economic growth, and related topics. But the original impetus for the work appears to have been criticism of the APP, particularly by Frank Knight, with whom Hayek engaged in debate (via journal articles) in the years 1933–1936. This debate is what is referred to as the second of the three "capital controversies."[16]

5.1 If Not the APP, Then What?

Though he came to disavow the APP, admitting that it was probably a bad idea to try to characterize any production process in terms of a single number in units of time, Hayek was at pains in a series of articles (among the most important of which are 1934, 1935, 1936a, and also 1941a) to strongly affirm the importance of time in production and investments decisions (plans), and, therefore, in explaining all aspects of the phenomenon of "capital," including notably its role in the Austrian business cycle. He wanted to expand the view beyond the simple Böhm-Bawerkian model of *Prices and Production* to take account of more complex cases, including durable capital goods, allowing for continuous input and output flows through time. Much of this was in the form of static equilibrium exercises, but, in his verbal remarks (as distinguished from the formal diagrammatic analysis) in the articles and in *The Pure Theory,* we find many valuable insights applicable to a dynamic world of continual change.

---

[15] "I rather hoped that what I'd done in capital theory would be continued by others.... . [Completing it myself] would have meant working for a result which I already knew, but I had to prove" (Hayek, 1994: 96; see also McClure et al., 2018, from where this quote is reproduced).

[16] The first capital controversy refers to the debate between Böhm-Bawerk and his critics, notably J. B. Clark. This controversy in many ways foreshadowed the second one. Böhm-Bawerk's particular conception of production using the APP was seen by Clark, as by Knight, as overly simplified, contradictory, and unhelpful in understanding the role of capital in the economy. Both Clark and Knight preferred a timeless conception of capital and production, where, in equilibrium, production and consumption are seen to be simultaneous, and speculations about "production periods" are beside the point. While Hayek never even came close to accepting this static equilibrium framework, except as a preliminary theoretical exercise, he did accept the criticisms of the APP, as we shall see.

As we noted earlier, Böhm-Bawerk's and Hayek's scheme (Tables 1 and 2 and Figures 3 and 4) can be viewed two ways, as a picture of the progress of a particular unit of input through time as it proceeds through the production process accumulating value (prospectively or retrospectively); or it can be seen as a snapshot of the various "stages of production" existing at a point of time in an ongoing production process producing output continuously. In a stationary world the two views look the same. What Hayek does in the 1934 and 1941 works is to express both simultaneously by adding a time dimension to the point of time perspective. We are asked to try to follow the progress through time of the whole array of inputs existing at every point in time. Instead of a single period to characterize a production process, Hayek identifies a function, "the time distribution of output due to a moment's input," that can be looked at two ways, as an *input function* that shows the share of the total input of a particular date represented in each date's output and by an *output function* showing the share of the total output over time of a single date's input represented in each date's output. The difference between the two functions (curves) in equilibrium represents the compound interest accrued and indicates the greater productivity of those processes that take "more time" (Hayek, 1934 and 1941a, chapters 8 and 9 and the editor's introduction, xxiii).

In place of a single APP, which would be quite complicated to calculate involving whole functions in the weights, Hayek refers to multiple *production periods*, or *investment periods*. Perhaps the most significant switch, within the thicket of multidimensional concepts, is the recognition that any metric of the amount of time involved in production cannot be independent of the rate of interest, something already evident in the simple APP with compound interest. As soon as this is realized, the notion of a single, invariant period of production disappears

> because the reinvestment of interest accrued up to any moment of time has to be counted as part of the total investment. It is for this reason ... that it is impossible to substitute any one-dimensional magnitude like "average period of production" for the concept of the investment function. For *there is no one single average period for which a quantity of factors could be invested with the result that the quantity of capital so created would be the same as if the same quantity of factors had been invested for the range of periods described by a given investment function, whatever the rate of interest. The mean value of these different investment periods which would satisfy this condition would have to be different for every rate of interest.* (Hayek, 1934: 86, italics added)

Nevertheless, even while having accepted this fact, Hayek attempted to preserve the implications of the ABCT that a fall in the money interest rate (the cost of investable funds) would lead on net, in equilibrium, to an increase in the number of "long" investment periods. He argued this in different ways in his work on capital theory in the 1930s (and even after when he returned briefly to a discussion of the Ricardo effect). He recognized that the input and output functions would not in general be invariant to changes in the interest rate (or, for that matter, to changes in technical knowledge or the demand for final output [the Keynesian concern], among other changes). Rather, an interest rate fall, for example, would cause a temporal reshuffling of inputs for the production of any set of outputs (and, indeed, may change the content of that set itself), *making the investment of any input earlier in the process more profitable*. He analyzed this case under the rubric of the "Ricardo effect" about which much discussion ensued (Hayek, 1939: 8–15; see Birner, 1999). In the case in which the money interest rate reduction was the result of money–credit expansion, and not an increase in savings, this reshuffling would prove to be largely unprofitable and unsustainable, producing the anatomy of the Austrian Business Cycle.[17]

The cases that Hayek investigates to motivate the idea that interest rate decreases can be shown to shift resources to early stages of production,[18] and similar effects, depend crucially on the simplifying assumptions he makes. They are illustrations of what *might* happen rather than of what *must* happen. It depends mostly on the shape of the input and output flows that constitute the investment in a manner familiar now from the arithmetic of the present value of cash flows in the financial literature. As Hayek puts it,

> So far it has been assumed that the shape of the productivity curve [flow of outputs at each date] of the factor in question in the different stages is the same. But this is not at all likely in practice. And *the actual effect of a change in the rate of interest on the price and distribution of any one factor will evidently depend on what we may call the relative interest elasticity of its productivity in the different stages* . . . the method adopted to give a general picture of the considerations involved is really not adequate for an exhaustive analysis. . . . if we were to start from a complete restatement of the substitution relationships between all the different resources concerned, all kinds of peculiarities and apparent anomalies would appear to be quite consistent with the general tendencies which can be deduced from a cruder type of analysis. It is, for instance, quite possible that while a fall in the rate of interest will create a tendency for the services of most of the permanent factors to be invested for longer periods and for their prices to rise, in the case

---

[17] By contrast, in case of an increase in the demand for the product, causing its price to rise (the real wage to fall), what may be seen as a "Keynesian" case, labor input will be redeployed toward the later stages of production.

[18] We should note that the shortcomings inherent in the notion of "stages of production" discussed in Section 4.2 apply with equal force in this context.

of some individual factor the effect may well be that it will be invested for shorter periods, or that its price will be lowered, or both." (1941a: 272, italics added, also quoted in Birner, 1999)[19]

In retrospect, perhaps the most significant part of all this was that Hayek was implicitly embracing a measure of "time in investment" that depended on the value of the investment itself, though, it seems that the full significance of this was not seen at the time. Specifically, it was not apparent to Hayek that a value construct was available to measure the average time one has to wait to earn a dollar on any investment – a construct that was a viable simple alternative to Böhm-Bawerk's APP, and that with this construct he could have addressed many of his concerns. We deal with this in detail in Section 9.6.

5.2 Capital Consumption and Maintenance: The Importance of Heterogeneity and Uncertainty

The recognition that any measure of time in investment depends on the rate of interest is an important instance of the more general dependence of any measure of capital on *the relative values of the production goods in question*. Hayek emphasizes that any relevant unforeseen changes will provoke changes in the *relative prices* of production goods and that this will in general lead to a reshuffling of the capital goods combinations being used in production processes. In other words, he recognizes the importance of *heterogeneity* in a way that anticipates the more systematic account of Ludwig Lachmann (discussed in the next section). But in his formal analysis of production process, for example his input and output functions and how they change, Hayek confines his attention to the "temporal" heterogeneity of the inputs. The same input at a different point of time is regarded as a different entity. Changes in the relative prices of these two entities provoke changes in their quantities (the amount of any input deployed at a point in time). In this formal part of his analysis, inputs are treated largely as homogeneous (labor services) at different points of time, applied to fixed (though heterogeneous) capital goods. A change in the relative prices of these inputs is, in effect, a change in intertemporal values, or equivalently, a change in the relevant interest (discount, accumulation) rate. In terms of the simple Böhm-Bawerkian framework, as depicted in Table 1, the contents

---

[19] Hayek here sees the possibility that changes in the interest rate may produce effects on the value of any investment, in terms of inputs and outputs, that are not monotonically related to those changes in the interest rate. Over some ranges that value may increase, and then decrease, and switch again, depending on the time distribution of the flow of services involved. This anticipates the main issue at the center of the third famous Cambridge-Cambridge debate, the third capital controversy of the 1960s, and beyond that we discuss briefly later in the Appendix.

of column 2, the physical inputs as well as input values inclusive of compound interest, are not invariant to the level of the interest rate.

In his general discussion Hayek clearly realizes the complex functional heterogeneity of production goods *at any point in time*, the clear and compelling implication of which is that there is no such thing as a "quantity of capital" independent of value, that is to say, in purely quantitative terms. This is the case in spite of the fact that Hayek, like many others, frequently refers to the "quantity" of capital, a practice that can be understood as coherent only if implicitly (and sometimes explicitly) referring to "a quantity in value terms." By often not being made explicit, this practice can lead to confusion and incoherence in encouraging the reader to think of capital in terms of some measurable (physical) quantity.[20]

That this is understood by Hayek is clear from his discussions of such topics as capital consumption, accumulation, and maintenance. Both Hayek and Mises were concerned during the 1920s and early 1930s about what they saw as the problem of capital consumption in Austria and wrote about it (see Hayek [1932] and the references therein). Hayek returned to this in the context of an exchange with A. C. Pigou (Hayek, 1935, 1941b, also 1941a, chapters 22 and 23; Pigou, 1935, 1941). This exchange is of particular relevance to an understanding of the Austrian approach to capital and to economics generally.

What does it mean to maintain the level of capital intact? Answering this one has to realize two fundamental truths:

1. As explained, there is no purely physical measure of capital. It is not even clear why one would want to keep capital intact in physical terms. Any useful measure of capital is a value measure. So maintaining capital means maintaining its *value*.
2. This being the case, we know that the capital value of any combination, or collection, of production goods is wholly determined by the present value of its prospective flow of valuable services. So keeping capital intact means maintaining its income stream in value terms. Capital is the stock from which income flows; the value of the stock is the (discounted) value of all of its flows.

As obvious (or maybe not?) as this might seem to us today, it is precisely around item number 1 that the disagreement between Hayek and Pigou revolved. This is perhaps best understood in terms of their different objectives. Pigou's primary concern, as part of his larger project on *The Economics of*

---

[20] A significant example is the neoclassical production function to be discussed briefly in Section 8.

Welfare (Pigou, 1932), was to understand *social income* (*national income, national dividend,* or what we would call today *GDP*). How could it be measured in a theoretically defensible way for practical use in economic policy, including facilitation of economic growth? To find such a measure it was necessary to account for those aggregate expenditures necessary to keep the productive capital resources of the nation intact. Hence his preoccupation with capital depletion, depreciation, and maintenance.

In pursuit of his investigations into *social income*, Pigou took an explicitly aggregative approach. He wanted to provide a measure (at least in principle) of the aggregate stock of capital of the economy and he looked to the *physical* items that comprised it for this purpose.

> [Pigou] starts with the proposition that, if the quantity of every unit in the nation's capital stock is unchanged over a period, then the total capital stock has been exactly maintained *even though its money value may have risen or fallen.* [This means that] changes in the general level of prices should not count as changes in the real capital stock for this purpose. ... changes in the value due to changes in rates of interest, which would alter the present discounted values of future receipts, should not count either. He also excluded changes in value due to changes in the quantity of labor working in conjunction with the capital stock, as well as changes due to shifts in *taste,* or to competition from *new equipment.* "In fact we may, I think, say quite generally, that all contractions in the money value of any parts of the capital stock that remain physically unaltered are irrelevant to the national dividend; and that their occurrence is perfectly compatible with the maintenance of capital intact" (Pigou [1946: 45]. (Scott, 1984: 60, italics added)

Regarding the physical characteristics of capital goods, Pigou distinguishes between natural changes of an extraordinary nature (such as war) and "normal" accidental changes (risks such as fire), excluding the former but including the latter in calculating necessary capital maintenance.

In proceeding in this way Pigou wants to argue that whereas an individual person or firm may experience changes in their volume of capital simply as a result of changes in their prices (values), this cannot, or may not, be true of the nation (the economy) as a whole. Relative price changes experienced by individuals will tend to "cancel out" so that the aggregate changes in value are not an accurate indication of changes in the volume of capital available for production. Thus, he wants to discover a measure of *real* capital behind the veil of individual valuations. Clearly, however, Pigou needed to find some way of adding up the heterogeneous capital goods and there is no way to do this except by finding a metric by which one capital good can be rendered commensurable with another, most obviously in terms of their contributions to the production of valuable items, in other words, to income and consumption. The various methods proposed by Pigou to accomplish this appear in retrospect to be rather forced.

It should be obvious that all of this would appear very problematic to Hayek, indeed methodologically unsound. An indication of how, at that time, mainstream economic perspectives on these matters were rapidly moving away from the perspectives of the Austrian economists, is given by looking at just how different Hayek's approach was and in what ways. For Hayek, and the Austrians, the aggregative approach makes little sense. In all economic reasoning one has to start from the individual and his evaluations. There was no sense in which one could talk of "social" income in a way that was disconnected from the incomes of the individuals who comprised the society. And to say that the one should balance out the capital gains of one against the losses of another in order to come to a measure of the income of the "society," and, indeed, to talk of the methods the national income statisticians should follow in calculating the maintenance expenditures to be deduced from social income to arrive at a measure of the net earnings of the society, would appear to be a meaningless exercise. The nation as such does not earn income or make decisions to maintain the capital it possesses; only individuals do, and Hayek was interested in these individual decisions, to be sure, in order to understand better how they factored into phenomena like business fluctuations and economic growth. It had to make sense for the individual decision-maker before its macro meanings and consequences could be deduced. And maintaining capital in purely physical terms made no sense for the individual income earner/ decision-maker.

Perhaps the most important illustration of this is the difference between physical *deterioration* and *obsolescence*. Though Pigou for the most part concentrates on the former, the *physical* life of the production good, when considering appropriate depreciation methods (maintenance planning), for Hayek as for us, it is solely the latter, the useful *economic* life of the production good, that is relevant. In most cases, for durable production goods, the economic life is likely to be shorter than the physical life. The good may have only scrap value once its usefulness in production has been superseded by a later, better version, or when a change in tastes and/or technology (for example, the introduction of a new consumer good) has reduced the demand for its services. (If the physical life is shorter than the hypothetical economic life were it physically able to continue in production, then the physical life is in effect the economic life – the good will have to be replaced at the end of its productive [physical] life.)

The matter was relevant to the Keynes–Hayek debate as well. As Horwitz (2011, 16) notes: "In the only real mention of the Austrian view of capital in The General Theory, Keynes (1936: 76) says:"

> It seems probable that capital formation and capital consumption, as used by the Austrian school of economists, are not identical either with investment and disinvestment as defined above or with net investment and disinvestment. In particular, capital consumption is said to occur in circumstances where there is quite clearly no net decrease in capital equipment as defined above. I have, however, been unable to discover a reference to any passage where the meaning of these terms is clearly explained. The statement, for example, that capital formation occurs when there is a lengthening of the period of production does not much advance matters.

Horwitz continues:

> Keynes's dismissiveness aside, this passage reveals much about the differences in approaches. Keynes seems puzzled by the Austrian claim that capital can be "consumed" even though there is no net decrease in physical capital. The answer to the puzzle is that capital, for the Austrians, is about value, not about the physical object itself. If we build a machine in anticipation of some specific future demand and then discover our expectations were wrong, the machine will drop in value (which is a form of capital consumption), but it does not crumple into dust. Capital goods are valued in terms of the (discounted) value of the future consumption goods they will produce. If consumer demand changes, the value of the capital good changes (assuming it is insufficiently versatile to produce whatever new product is now in demand) and capital-value is lost, thus capital has been consumed even though the physical stock of capital has not changed. This [is important in any] discussion of the business cycle. (Horwitz, 2011: 16)

The appropriate procedure for the individual producer (or owner of durable goods combinations generally) who wants to maintain a given level of production (revenue income) is to anticipate as best she can the economic life of the production components of the project and to provide for their physical maintenance, replacement, training, etc. so as to achieve this. That, according to Hayek, is what we should mean when we talk of keeping our capital intact. Accordingly, one of the key conclusions is that "'the stock of capital required to keep income from any moment onwards constant cannot in any sense be defined as a constant magnitude" Hayek, 1935: 181). This prompts some very interesting questions for students of ACT. The key question is what does maintaining a given level of income mean? As capital is a means to an end, the end being income (utility), maintaining capital must imply maintaining income. So the question gets "pushed back" – what do we mean by a constant income?

5.3 Permanent Income: What Is Foreseen and What Is Not Foreseen

In an article published in 1942 (the substance of which was explicitly reproduced and reaffirmed 30 years later in his *Capital and Time* [1973, note to
chapter XIII]), John Hicks proposed a resolution between Hayek and Pigou on
the question of the maintenance of capital (Hicks, 1942). This resolution ran
along the lines of suggesting that while Hayek was essentially correct in
demolishing Pigou's approach and explaining the essentials of a defensible
approach (namely, one based firmly on the perceptions and expectations of
individual producer/entrepreneur), Hayek had not offered anything of practical
use for the purposes of social accounting.[21] Hicks then proceeded to offer his
own approach, which need not concern us here.

Both he and Hayek use Hicks's important definition of income in this
context, which Hicks had described and lucidly analyzed in *Value and
Capital* (1939, chapter XIV), which has become the standard reference on the
subject, namely, "the idea of income as *the maximum rate of consumption
which the recipient can enjoy and expect to continue to enjoy indefinitely*"
(Scott, 1984: 62, italics added), sometimes referred to as "Hicksian income,"
but called by Hayek, the now more standard, *permanent income*. In *Value and
Capital* Hicks had expressed misgivings about this concept insofar as it renders
the concepts of saving, depreciation, and investment, not "suitable tools for
any analysis which aims at logical precision. There is far too much equivocation in their meaning, equivocation which cannot be removed by the most
painstaking effort. At bottom, they are not logical categories at all; they are
rough approximations, used by the businessman to steer himself through the
bewildering changes of situation which confront him. For this purpose, strict
logical categories are not what is needed; something rougher is actually better"
(1939: 171; quoted also in Scott 1984). In other words, the concept was too
subjective for this liking.[22] But certainly not for Hayek's.

Using this concept of permanent income, Hayek analyzes cases of increasing
complexity and uncertainty. In a stationary world in which the future can be
accurately foreseen, including any developments that would render any productive resources economically obsolete, the problem of maintaining capital

---

[21] "Professor Hayek, on the other hand, having demolished the rival construction, fails (in my
view) to provide anything solid to put in its place" (Hicks, 1942: 174). Even in the most
"subjectivist" (Austrian, Mengerian) period of his career (save for his early "Hayekian"
phase) from the mid-1970s onward, Hicks remained wedded to the need to use stationary-
state reasoning to discover constructs of use for aggregate reasoning (and by implication
economic policy?). See Lewin (1997).

[22] Hicks: "'calculations of social income...play...an important part in social statistics, and in
welfare economics" (1939: 180).

intact is a purely technical one that takes on a high degree of objectivity. The simplest case is probably the one we find in *Prices and Production*, illustrated in Table 2 and in Figure 3, bearing in mind that along with everything else, interest rate changes are correctly foreseen, and all technical production conditions are known with certainty. In such a world, the amount of input in each period necessary to ensure the largest constant output value can be easily calculated and applied as necessary to ensure a constant flow of permanent income. The division between maintenance and production is somewhat arbitrary, but any accounting convention consistently applied to this end will suffice to define the amount necessary for capital maintenance. This is the essence of many neoclassical growth models that assume a constant depreciation rate that has to be subtracted from the compound interest rate to derive a sustainable growth path.

One can fairly easily see the consequences of relaxing these highly restrictive assumptions and allowing uncertainty regarding obsolescence, demand shifts (market conditions), and even technical conditions. The problem then becomes a highly subjective one. Expectations relating to these matters will differ across individuals. The producer/entrepreneur has to pit his bet, his expectations, against those of others. The idea of an objectively identifiable depreciation rate or income level is untenable. Hayek notes that the producer will try to take into account in his calculations and his actions in dividing his earnings between consumption and maintenance all those relevant events that are foreseeable (in any degree). But for those that are unforeseeable this cannot be done – and Hayek might well have added that to model the situation as if this were not the case (for the purposes of social accounting or any other purpose) is a pretence of knowledge.[23]

In addition to these difficulties, it should be noted that, unlike Hayek's triangle situation, the flow of inputs may vary over time and that for any estimate of permanent income there may be multiple quantity-time inputs to achieve it; in other words, there may be different amounts of expenditure in each subperiod of production (the entries in column 2 of Table 1) devoted to maintenance that would achieve the same permanent income level, so that even understood as the result of subjective calculation, the expenditure level (and time pattern) required for maintenance may not be unique.

---

[23] "In a world of imperfect foresight not only the size of the capital stock, but also the income derived from it will inevitably be subject to unintended and unpredictable changes which depend on the extent and distribution of foresight, and there will be no possibility of distinguishing any particular movement of these magnitudes as normal" (Hayek, 1935: 181). Furthermore, the occurrence of the unexpected, the unforeseen, features prominently in any Hayekian explanation of economic fluctuations. The over-and then under-maintenance of capital is of the essence of a boom–bust cycle, one that leaves the economy with less capital in its wake.

Finally, the use of permanent income as a standard for comprehending capital maintenance is purely a convention, though an intuitive one. In a growing economy it may make more sense to think in terms of a permanent rate of growth of income, or constant per capita income, as the relevant standard. And in the individual context, the producer's objective may be one that entails a nonconstant income (output) or even nonconstant growth rate. This requires a more flexible and complex calculation of what his level of consumption in each period should be and what his investments of inputs should be in order to achieve this.

Hicks's observation that in his relentless demolition of the idea of capital maintenance as a purely technical matter subject to certain articulable procedures, Hayek has left "nothing solid" on which the economist might build, might perhaps be countered, along the lines of Mises's approach to capital (to be discussed in the text that follows) that it is *precisely* because of the subjective nature of capital, permanent income, and related concepts that *the conventions of accounting practice and financial calculation* are so important and useful. The dynamic economy in which we live is crucially dependent on the smooth functioning of the institution of money and no less the institutions of accounting and finance *using monetary values.*

These institutions facilitate decision-making. The ability to use financial arithmetic within an accounting framework provides the producer (entrepreneur) the wherewithal to calculate according to her best estimates the profitability of the productive venture at hand. In acting on these estimates which will over time be revealed to have been right or wrong, to some degree, and this will prompt changes going forward, but in their absence she *would not have been able to make a decision at all and would not have acted.*[24] In the absence of these institutions, which exist only in a for-profit private-property economy, no market process would exist, no trial and error speculation/investment that is the key to social learning. Hayek's 1935 article in particular[25] (together with

---

[24] This is consistent with both Hayek's later preoccupation with the function and development of all manner of "social institutions" and with his epistemological concerns relating to the subjective content of individual plans (Hayek, 1937). Institutions such as money, finance, and accounting provide the individual planner with shared categories that enable her to act in an uncertain world. A simple example is the preparation of a business plan to use as the basis for obtaining a business loan, and for reporting on the use of funds so obtained. Financial markets functioning at a high level depend on these institutions.

[25] It appears plausible to us that this 1935 article was very important in the development of subsequent contributions by Ludwig Lachmann, and perhaps others, toward a dynamic vision of capital with heterogeneity and change at its center. We say this notwithstanding Lachmann's statement referring to Hayek (1937b): "The ideas set forth by Professor Hayek have been the main inspiration of this paper" (Lachmann, 1948: 308n). In fact Hayek (1937b) is less directly relevant to these questions. Lachmann may be referring most to the implications of its title. See Lewin (2013).

similar work from this period) is an important complement to both Lachmann's discussion of point of time capital-good heterogeneity and Mises's financial approach to capital.

6 Ludwig Lachmann's Kaleidic World of Capital Heterogeneity

As a result of the ambiguities in the concept of capital, Hayek attempted in the 1930s to find a more satisfactory way of conceptualizing the capital structure. This protracted project culminated in the publication of *The Pure Theory of Capital* (1941), an elaborate though unsatisfactory conclusion to the attempt to construct a dynamic theory of capital. Ludwig Lachmann, a student of Hayek's at the London School of Economics, had begun working on the problem in the 1940s and developed a different approach. This work was ultimately crystallized in his *Capital and Its Structure* (1956). Lachmann's capital theory provides the definitive understanding of the nature and working of the capital structure for Austrians today. Rather than conceiving of production as involving a homogeneous mass of "capital" as a stock (as in both the neoclassical and modern Ricardian conceptions), Lachmann sees it as involving an ordered structure of heterogeneous multispecific complementary production goods. This structure is ever changing as entrepreneurs combine and recombine productive resources in accordance with their assessments of profitability. Profit and loss continually reshapes the production structure in accordance with the revealed preferences of consumers. One may contend that Lachmann, like Mises in a different way (Section 7), closed the circle back to the original vision of Carl Menger.

6.1 The Heterogeneity of Production Goods and the Austrian School

Although Böhm-Bawerk's APP has no defensible application to real-world production processes, the essential idea is important and is a precursor to much work on the nature of production in the modern world[26]. Böhm-Bawerk tried to capture in quantitative terms the average amount of time taken in any production project – and from this it was but a small step to seeing it as a purely physical measure of physical capital. His approach invites the interpretation that time is a metric for reducing heterogeneous capital goods (production goods) to a common denominator. In a sense capital is time, production time.

Lachmann maintained that, outside of equilibrium, there was simply no way to aggregate the bewildering array of heterogeneous production goods. In

---

[26] For example, one can find in Böhm-Bawerk's capital theory precursors of both the heterogeneous structure idea and the credit-induced business cycle idea that became ABCT.

reality capital was not a stock of anything. It was, rather, a structure of different things fitting together to serve the purposes of their employers.

In a now famous quote, Lachmann explains:

> The generic concept of capital without which economists cannot do their work has no measurable counterpart among material objects; it reflects the entrepreneurial appraisal of such objects. Beer barrels and blast furnaces, harbor installations and hotel room furniture are capital not by virtue of their physical properties but by virtue of their economic functions. Something is capital because the market, the consensus of entrepreneurial minds, regards it as capable of yielding an income ... [though heterogeneous in nature] the stock of capital used by society does not present a picture of chaos. Its arrangement is not arbitrary. There is some order to it. (Lachmann, 1956, xv)

According to Lachmann, though the capital stock is heterogeneous, it is not amorphous. The various components of the capital structure stand in a sensible relationship to one another because they perform *specific* functions together. They are used in various capital combinations. If we understand the logic of capital combinations, we give meaning to the capital structure and, in this way, we are able to design appropriate economic policies or, even more importantly, avoid inappropriate ones (for example, Lachmann, 1947, 1956:123).

Understanding capital combinations entails an understanding of the concepts of *complementarity* and *substitutability*. These concepts pertain to a world in which perceived prices are actual (disequilibrium) prices, in the sense that they reflect inconsistent expectations and in which changes that occur cause protracted visible adjustments. Capital goods are complements if they contribute together to a given *production plan*. A production plan is defined by the pursuit of a given set of ends to which the production goods are the means. As long as the plan is being successfully fulfilled, all of the production goods stand in complementary relationship to one another. They are part of the same plan. The complementarity relationships within the plan may be quite intricate and no doubt will involve different stages of production and distribution.

Substitution occurs when a production plan fails (in whole or in part). When some element of the plan fails, a contingency adjustment must be sought. Thus, some resources must be substituted for others. This is the role, for example, of spare parts or excess inventory. Thus, complementarity and substitutability are properties of different states of the world. The same good can be a complement in one situation and a substitute in another.[27] Substitutability can be gauged

---

[27] Lachmann uses the example of a delivery company (Lachmann, 1947: 199; and Lachmann, 1956 [1978]: 56). The company possesses a number of delivery vans. Each one is a complement to the others in that they cooperate to fulfill an overall production plan. That plan encompasses the routine completion of a number of different delivery routes. As long as the plan is being

only to the extent that a certain set of contingency events can be visualized. There may be some events, such as those caused by significant technological changes, that, not having been predictable, render some production plans valueless. The resources associated with them will have to be incorporated into some other production plan or else scrapped—they will have been rendered unemployable. This is a natural result of economic progress that is driven primarily by the trial-and-error discovery of new and superior outputs and techniques of production. What determines the fate of any capital good in the face of change is the extent to which it can be fitted into any other capital combination without loss in value. The extent to which it can maintain its value in alternative combinations is a measure of its degree of substitutability. Capital goods are regrouped. Those that lose their value completely are scrapped. That is, capital goods, though heterogeneous and diverse, are often capable of performing a number of different economic functions. They are multispecific.

Within the plan of a single organization the production goods may appear in a *planned complementary* relationship to one another. This is the role of the entrepreneur, to form and reform profitable capital combinations. At a higher level the different plans of different production organizations (firms) exhibit an *unplanned complementarity* that is the result of the market process. It is a spontaneous order brought about by the functioning of the price system providing profit and loss signals and incentives.

As Bill Tulloh points out, *degree of specificity* can be thought of as another "dimension" in relation to capital goods. Capital goods are economic goods by virtue of the *purpose* they are made to serve by the entrepreneur. Money is the least specific, most general, while some have multiple possible purposes all the way to those that have only a single purpose. Money may be thought of as a kind of "general purpose technology." Money is *specified* into concrete capital goods.[28]

6.2 Heterogeneity, Investment, and Technological Change

Lachmann's work on capital occurred in the context of Keynesian revolution. He was at the time at the London School of Economics, the center of the Hayekian opposition to the Cambridge Keynesians. In a 1948 article he specifically discusses the implications of his view of capital for Keynes's approach.

---

fulfilled, this relationship prevails, but if one of the vans should break down, one or more of the others may be diverted in order to compensate for the unexpected loss of the use of one of the productive resources. To that extent and in that situation, they are substitutes.

[28] Personal communication gratefully acknowledged.

> The modern theory of investment, set forth by Lord Keyes in *The General Theory,* has had its many triumphs these last twelve years, but it still has a number of gaps. Conceiving of investment as simple growth of a stock of homogeneous capital, it is ill-equipped to cope with situations in which the immobility of heterogeneous capital resources imposes a strain on the economic system. In particular, it can tell us little about the "inducement to invest" in a world where scarcity of some capital resources co-exists with abundance of others. (Lachmann, 1948: 131)

In this article (1948) Lachmann then proceeds to lay out a detailed analysis of the implications of capital heterogeneity, perhaps even more fully and clearly than in his earlier 1947 article on complementarity and substitutability. He links these concepts to the theory of investment (which he points out must contain an implicit theory of capital) and specifically to Keynes's marginal efficiency concept (which lacks any recognition of such a theory). Anticipating his future preoccupations, he also explores the role of changing and inconsistent expectations and points out that this implies the enduring existence of disequilibrium.

6.3 Capital Accumulation Usually Entails Technological Change

Perhaps the most important general implication of a disequilibrium approach to capital is the proposition that capital accumulation very often entails technological change. Most technical change is embodied in new (improved) capital goods and/or involves the production of new consumption goods. It is very likely that government expenditure "crowds out" not only private sector investment but also private sector investment-induced technical progress. The shape of the capital structure will be different and, because capital assets are heterogeneous, specific, and durable, will remain different from what it would otherwise have been.

   Given that capital accumulation and technological progress go together, Lachmann recasts Böhm-Bawerk's intuition about increasing roundaboutness into the idea of increasing *complexity*. Production goods are heterogeneous and exist in a structure of production that becomes more complex and heterogeneous with economic progress. Lachmann's theory is a theory of progress reflected in and achieved by a continuing specialization of economic activities, a growing division of function. Heterogeneity matters because heterogeneous capital goods perform *qualitatively* different functions and they do so in combination with other human and physical resources.

   New goods, new methods of production, new modes of organization, new resources (production-goods) (Schumpeter, 1942: 84–85) – all of these are part of the market process, all this change is part of the "information age." It is not simply the fact of changes in technology that is revolutionary; it is the speed with which it is occurring that is new. The pace of change is not only quicker; it is accelerating. Lachmann's considerations suggest, however, that our ability to absorb and adjust to change has dramatically increased; it must have, or else we would not be able to observe these changes, occurring as they do within a well-ordered social framework, a framework that remains intact in spite of the ubiquity and accelerating speed of change.

To understand the phenomenon of accelerating structural change occurring together with our enhanced abilities to adapt to change, we must realize that *the scope and pace of technological change is governed by our ability to generate and process relevant information.* This means that the current pace of technical change is dependent on the results of past technical advances, particularly the ability to generate and process information. This is a complex process involving multilevel interactions over time. If technological change is seen as the result of many trial-and-error selections (of production processes, of product types, of modes of distribution, and so on) then the ability to generate and perceive more possibilities will result in a greater number of successes. It will, of course, also result in a greater number of failures. Lachmann's proposition that capital accumulation, proceeding as it does hand in hand with technological change, necessarily brings with it capital regrouping as a result of failed production plans, appears in this perspective to be particularly pertinent.

6.4 Lachmann's Contributions to ACT in Relation to "Capital as Finance"

A central motif in Lachmann's work is the advance in Austrian economics toward a framework that is satisfactorily subjective. Born with the affirmation that value is subjective, the next important step for the Austrians was the affirmation that expectations are subjective, and, being so, were necessary divergent across people. This is no more true than in the theory of capital.

While it is true that Lachmann's (like Hayek's) discussions in capital theory are preoccupied with physical, objective, production processes and the resources they involve, the implicit message throughout is about the *value* of these resources as organized and deployed by the producer-entrepreneur. Profit is the objective. And to earn profit value must be added to the resources in the form of an income stream from the output they produce. This is what makes anything part of "capital" rather than simply a physical object. The value attributed to any production good is the projection of the subjective appraisal by the entrepreneur of its potential to produce (together with complementary resources) something of value greater than what it costs to acquire and use.

There is a clear connection between a consideration of the physical form of the capital structure and the notion of profitability.

Having said this, it remains true, that Lachmann (like Hayek, but unlike Mises, as we show in the next section), is not explicit about the notion of "capital" as distinct from "capital goods" and, although there is some discussion of financial assets in *Capital and its Structure* (1956, chapter 6), he does not spell out clearly the role of financial calculation (for example, present value estimation) by the decision-maker. In this he is no different from most of the Austrians. Where they do mention it is always in passing. The clearest statement by Lachmann is perhaps the following:

> ... capital-goods have a *value dimension* as well as their physical dimension. While in terms of the latter capital is of course heterogeneous, in terms of the former divers capital-goods may be *reduced to homogeneity*. In fact, in planning and carrying out plans *this has to be done since the planner has to match means with ends* and, except for sums of money, almost all his means are capital-goods. He has to *evaluate* them in order to make them commensurable to each other as well as to his ends. Every plan, simply for the sake of the comparability of the means it employs, has to *assign values* to its capital inputs. Plan failure and consequent revision will probably entails changes in the evaluation of capital-goods, but it is a peculiar aspect of our problem that even while the plan proceeds satisfactorily with no unexpected change in the workshop or market, planers may have reason to change capital-values. Changes in the value dimension may not be accompanied by any other observable event. (Lachmann, 1986: 79, italics added)

Earlier he says: "We might say of course that the firm will act in such a manner as to maximize the present-value of its expected future income stream, "but immediately adds, "but such a description ... is of little use to us" (Lachmann, 1986: 64).

In addition, in his consideration of the phenomenon of *capital maintenance*, Lachmann adopts an approach (citing Hayek, 1935) that entails keeping the capitalized *value* of the expected income stream intact. This implies using a value approach to the estimation of depreciation and resort to accounting and financial conventions. In somewhat confusing terminology, Lachmann explains as follows: "Capital could be said to maintain its quantity while altering its form only if the maintenance of its value, while it is embodied in each of these forms, could be assured" (Lachmann, 1986: 71) and further, "Maintaining the value of capital resources is an important economic function" (Lachmann, 1986: 73).

Conceiving of capital in this way, as the result of a subjective evaluation process of productive resources, compels a consideration of the nature of productive labor, or, what we today call human capital. Lachmann, again in common with the other Austrians, never uses this term, nor considers human capital in the same analytical category as physical capital. Passing statements do, however, indicate his awareness of the issue. For example:

> It goes without saying that in the real world it will hardly be possible to produce a new good, or vary effectively the character of an existing one, without varying the *blend of skills required* in the labor force, or the composition of raw material input used. Similarly, any change in the latter or the *composition of the labor force* is bound to have some effect on output. But it is no less true that there can be hardly and significant change in output or labor or raw material input which does not necessitate a regrouping of the capital combination with or without new investment. (Lachmann, 1986: 64–65, italics added; see also Lachmann, 1956: 49)

It should be clear that from the perspective of the decision-maker evaluating productive resources in general that there is no *categorical* difference between physical and human resources. There are of course enormous *practical* differences associated with their employment and management, given that human resources have agency and dealing with them entails forming a relationship that is absent in the case of the employment of physical resources. But in terms of calculating the capital value of the firm and its "capital combinations" the potential contributions of labor (the human capital available to it) have to be included in the same way as those of physical production goods.

Relating to the broader framework adopted in this Element, Lachmann's work adds considerable detail to the second text box from the left concerning the purchase and rental of heterogeneous, complementary resources, in Figure 2.[29]

7 Ludwig von Mises's "Capital from a Financial Perspective"

7.1 Mises Has a Financial View of Capital

Ludwig von Mises never produced a work devoted solely to an exploration of the meaning of capital or its role in the economy. Other Austrian school economists such as Böhm-Bawerk (1890), Hayek (1941a), Lachmann (1956), and Kirzner (1966) all published books on the subject, in addition to numerous articles. Mises's views must be gleaned from his remarks in works devoted to other specific or general topics. He did not enter into any "capital controversy" or specifically consider them. Yet, his views on capital are interesting and highly suggestive in a way that we believe has been generally

---

[29] See the excellent discussion relevant to Lachmann's entrepreneur as a financial calculator in Horwitz (2011: 13–14).

underappreciated. In particular, Mises seems to be something of an outlier within the Austrian school when it comes to capital – though his position is arguably foreshadowed in a neglected article by Menger (1888).

Only very recently has the issue of a dissenting view on capital by the older Carl Menger been noted (Braun, 2015a,b). In this article Menger opposed all attempts to define capital as something physical. He considered it necessary to stick with common terminology where capital relates to sums of money dedicated to the acquisition of income. But, having come this far, Menger does not do much more than criticize other definitions of capital, opting for the abandonment of physical capital concepts in economics.

In particular, he does not indicate what a capital theory that is based on the financial capital concept he endorses would look like (Braun, 2015a: 91).

Of the later Austrians, only Mises based his discussion of capital on Menger's (1888) financial capital concept. Both in his treatise on socialism (Mises, 1922: 123) and in his magnum opus, *Human Action*, Mises (1949: 262), he stuck to the more common understanding of capital and chose to orient his definition of capital to business practice. For him, capital is a sum of money which is determined by accounting. As previously quoted:

> Capital is the sum of the money equivalent of all assets minus the sum of the money equivalent of all liabilities as dedicated at a definite date to the conduct of the operations of a definite business unit. It does not matter in what these assets may consist, whether they are pieces of land, buildings, equipment, tools, goods of any kind and order, claims, receivables, cash, or whatever. (Mises, 1949: 262)

To Mises, it is not physical characteristics that determine whether assets are part of capital or not. Of primary interest is rather which role they play in the operations of business units (Lewin, 1998). Thus, Mises, together with Menger (1888), deviates from the majority view of the Austrian school on capital. Different from Menger (1888), however, Mises (1920, 1922, 1949) actually contains several hints as to what a capital theory based on a financial capital concept would look like.

7.2 Ambiguities in Mises's View of Capital

Mises does not abandon the contributions of his predecessors to the Austrian theory of (physical) capital. He elaborates at quite some length on Böhm-Bawerk's trade-off between longer periods of production, characterized by additional higher-order goods and the demand for consumption (Mises, 1949: 476–480). He talks about Böhm-Bawerk's APP and the problems attached to it and of the difficulties in general of calibrating time in production (Mises, 1949:

476–480 and various other places). He differs from Böhm-Bawerk and most other Austrians in that he tries to separate these "physical" considerations from the theory of capital. His lengthy treatment may have caused confusion – or at least failed to clear up existing confusions because of the terminological choice he makes at the outset of his discussion of capital to refer to production goods as *capital goods*.

After he has presented his definition of capital as the money value of the assets and liabilities of a business unit, he investigates the physical capital concept employed by most other economists. But although he considers physical capital, defined as "the totality of the produced factors of production," to be "an empty concept" and a "mythical" notion, he nonetheless, with some apprehension, calls these factors "*capital goods*" (Mises, 1949: 263). These goods are, in his (1949: 490) words, "intermediary stations on the way leading from the very beginning of production to its final goal, the turning out of consumers' goods." That he is well aware of the problematic nature of this terminology can be seen in the very sentences where he introduces the concept: "We may *acquiesce* in the terminological usage of calling the produced factors of production capital-goods. *But this does not render the concept of real [physical] capital any more meaningful*" (Mises, 1949: 263, italics added). Again, Mises (1949: 260, italics added) is clearly aware that it is very important not to confuse (financial) capital and physical capital goods: "From the notion of *capital-goods* one must clearly distinguish the concept of *capital*. The concept of capital is *the fundamental concept of economic calculation, the foremost mental tool of the conduct of affairs in the market economy*." Despite these unambiguous statements, historians of economic thought and other Austrian economists have not given much weight to his distinctive definition of capital. His definition, which clearly aims at a financial capital concept, has not been made much use of by later Austrian economists. In part this may be due to Mises in another place (Mises, 1949: 512) suggesting that capital is a praxeological category rather than an historically contingent one – being peculiar to the institutional environment of capitalism that we discuss in the text that follows (see Braun et al., 2016: 856–857).

And in another place he writes the following:

> There is no such thing as an abstract or ideal capital that exists apart from concrete capital-goods. . . . we must realize that capital is always embodied in definite capital-goods and is affected by everything that happens with regard to them. The value of an amount of capital is a derivative of the value of the capital-goods in which it is embodied. The money equivalent of an amount of capital is the sum of the money equivalents of the aggregate of capital-goods to which one refers in speaking of capital in the abstract. . . .

> Capital is always in the form of definite capital-goods. These capital-goods are better utilizable for some purposes, less utilizable for others, and absolutely useless for still other purposes. (Mises, 1949: 500)

This may seem to contradict his earlier definitions. Mises's discussion here is all about the degree of *specificity* of *capital-goods*, the distinction between "free" and "fixed" capital and the significance and validity of these distinctions. And in this regard, he talks not only about the distinction between capital and capital goods, but also about the *connection* between them, as in the foregoing quote, "Capital is always *in the form* of definite capital-goods" (italics added). Mises is here using a confusing terminology. It seems that what he wants to say is that the (financial) capital of any business is embodied in *business assets* – without them there is no capital in the business to speak of. *Capital goods* instead of *business assets* or *productive resources* may constitute a part of what is valued by "capital" but not necessarily the whole of it. Notably, consideration of how human capital is related to capital value is neglected.

In an earlier essay where Mises deals with the phenomena of heterogeneous capital goods and malinvestment, and with the "consequences [that] are brought about by limitations in the convertibility of *fixed capital*" (Mises, 1931: 233, italics added).We see Mises dealing here with the *relationship* between financial capital and the physical production goods to which capital is connected historically and through time. His use of phrases like "fixed capital" or "free capital" invites confusion. But, notice the distinction between "individual capital-goods" and "true capital" in the following quotation.

> [O]nly "true capital", in Clark's sense, has mobility, but ... individual capital-goods do not. Capital goods, as produced material factors of production, are intermediary steps on the way toward a definite goal—a consumer's good. If in the course of the period of production subsequent changes in the entrepreneur's goals are caused by a change in the data of the market, the intermediary products already available cannot always be used for the attainment of the new goals. This holds true both of goods of fixed and goods of circulating capital, although in greater measure of the former. Capital has mobility in so far as it is technologically possible to transfer individual capital-goods from one branch of production to another or to transport them from one location to another. (Mises, 2003, original publication date 1931, 232, footnote reference to J. B. Clark omitted)

Though admittedly potentially confusing, it makes sense to understand this as referring to capital in the sense of capital value being mobile only insofar as the *capital goods* from which such capital value derives are multispecific, that is, can be adapted to various uses other than those for which they are currently employed. It is perhaps understandable then that later authors have mostly ignored Mises's approach to capital. Although he is mostly clear that capital goods in themselves and by themselves are not capital and that only as *business* assets does their money value become capital, what he says can be and has been interpreted as an elaboration on earlier Austrian work on the role of capital goods in the production process, which, in part, it is, but within his particular view of capital as a financial, accounting mental tool for business calculation and decision-making.

It should be noted that there is some disconnect between the concepts of capital being the market value of all goods used in the production process regardless of their shape and form on one hand, and capital being the market value of assets minus liabilities on the other. The latter refers to the equity in a balance sheet of the firm. However, a good used in the production process can be financed by the owner of the firm (equity) or through a loan (liabilities). The *source* of the financial funds does not define the *use* of the good in question. While we have sympathy for Mises's approach to define capital as a market value rather than constrained set of goods (only capital goods), it would be more precise to define capital as the market value of the assets used in production, rather than narrow this term only to equity.

7.3 Mises's Capital Is an Historically Specific Concept

Capital, in Mises's view, is a basic and indispensable tool of economic calculation used by entrepreneurs in capitalist economies, that is, in market economies. He clearly considers it as an *historically specific* concept:

> The concept of capital cannot be separated from the context of monetary calculation and from the social structure of a market economy in which alone monetary calculation is possible. It is a concept which makes no sense outside the conditions of a market economy. It plays a role exclusively in the plans and records of individuals acting on their own account in such a system of private ownership of the means of production, and it developed with the spread of economic calculation in monetary terms. (Mises, 1949: 262)

Monetary calculation based on capital is possible only under capitalism. Owing to the tools of *capital accounting*, entrepreneurs are able to compare the economic significance of their inputs and their outputs even in a complicated and dynamically "changing industrial economy" (Mises, 1949: 511). That is what distinguishes capitalism from other economic systems: "[O]nly people who are in a position to resort to monetary calculation can evolve to full clarity the distinction between an economic substance [capital] and the advantages derived from it [income], and can apply it neatly to all classes, kinds, and orders of goods and services" (Mises, 1949: 261).Mises's theory of capital is a theory of the way monetary calculation based on (financial) capital helps entrepreneurs to organize the production process under capitalism. One could also say that his theory of capital is a theory of capitalism, a theory of how entrepreneurial operations are guided by capital accounting.

It may be argued that Mises's take on the theory of capital as finance is only rudimentary and needs further elaboration (see, e.g., Braun, 2015b). In this, he is in the company of other economists who adopted a financial capital concept (notably Frank Fetter [1977, collected essays from early in the twentieth century] and Irving Fisher [1906]). And, indeed, we shall attempt to articulate some of the detail that we believe is logically part of a fuller financial approach to capital. What is perhaps unique in Mises, however, is his use of an understanding of what capital is, and must be to provide a critique of socialism. Without the institutions of monetary calculation, it would not be possible to reduce inputs and outputs to a common denominator and an industrial economy would not be sustainable. Hence, the impossibility under socialism to economize on resources and to determine where input factors can be employed most economically: "[I]t lies in the very nature of socialist production that the shares of the particular factors of production in the national dividend cannot be ascertained, and that it is impossible in fact to gauge the relationship between expenditure [production effort] and income [production proceeds]" (Mises, 1920: 2; brackets contain translations by Braun in Braun et al., 2016). A socialist government would badly need what the capitalist system has, namely the concepts of capital and income to guide its operations. However, without private ownership in the means of production, without markets and prices for such goods, the concepts of capital and income are "mere postulates devoid of any practical application" (Mises, 1949, 264; see also the excellent discussion in Murphy, 2015: 223–246).

Mises's discussion of capital is a discussion of how the institutions of monetary calculation work and how far they contribute to a rational allocation of production factors in capitalism. For Mises, as for us, capital is a mental tool that is necessary for understanding the modern world.

8 Capital in the Aggregate Production Function

8.1 A Böhm-Bawerkian Production Function?

In the postwar period attention drifted away from "Austrian-style" (perhaps Euro-style is better) capital theory that involved detailed considered of the role to time in production and investment. The Keynesian revolution established macroeconomics as legitimate sub-branch of economic inquiry focusing on the relationship between aggregates. If time featured at all it was in discerning time lapses between the movements of the aggregates. A sub-branch for this new area of study was growth theory. The seminal articles are Solow (1956) and Swan (1956), spurring an enormous, still growing, literature on the Solow–Swan (neoclassical) growth model. An economy's ability to grow depended on its productive resources, labor and capital. Population was mostly regarded as exogenous, and labor was considered to be fully employed so all of the work was done by capital accumulation (investment was understood to be the addition to capital). In recent years the model was augmented by endogenous population growth, human capital, and external effects (social capital). Technological change was considered mostly exogenous, but some recent endogenous aspects such as the return to investments in research and development have been added on occasion. This neoclassical production function is the workhorse of much of modern literature on economic development and related topics.[30]

A valuable by-product of the theory was its ability, using the marginal productivity framework, to explain the distribution of output (income) between capital and labor. It is not surprising, therefore, that this approach attracted a strong Marxist influence, in addition to the neoclassical core. During the 1960s and following, the neoclassical production function was the object of attack by the "Cambridge Marxists" UK (neo-Ricardians) against the "Cambridge Massachusetts" neoclassicals, on the presumption that it was essential to the validity of the marginal productivity explanation of the distribution of income (that is, that the earnings of resource owners [factors of production] could be explained according to the employers' estimations of the values of the marginal products of the resources employed) and that demolishing the notion of capital upon which the aggregate production function depended, they would, at the same time, demolish the marginal productivity theory of distribution. The neo-Ricardians were correct in their criticism of the aggregate production function, but for the wrong reasons, and demolishing the basis upon which it rested, does not invalidate the marginal productivity of distribution. We discuss this in the Appendix.

The logic of the production function is widely known and need not be explained in detail here. Less well known perhaps is one interpretation of Böhm-Bawerk's framework that gave rise to a particular version of the production function fully compatible with its general form. The most well known is

---

[30] Most recently, it was the instrument used by Thomas Piketty (2014) in his widely noted work. Picketty has a narrow view of capital that he uses in a simple production function framework to derive implications about the distribution of income and wealth. For a critique of this work related to our topic see Lewin and Cachanosky (2018c).

perhaps Dorfman (1959a; see also Dorfman, 1959b, 2001 and Fabre, 1979). Here is an example from Dorfman (1959a).

> Consider, now, a stationary economy whose period of production is p. Let N denote the labor force and w the annual wage rate. Then goods incorporating labor valued at Nw are produced each year, and goods incorporating labor valued at Nwp are produced each period. We can at once calculate the value of the labor which must be tied up in the capital stock of the economy at any time in order to achieve these levels of output, wages and employment. In each time interval dt (small or large) production is completed on goods that incorporate labor valued at $Nwdt$. Assume, now, that labor is expended on goods at a steady rate so that goods started up t years ago have incorporated in them the fraction t/p of their ultimate labor cost. Then goods started up in the time interval t years ago to $t + dt$ years ago incorporate at present labor valued at $Nw(tip)dt$. And, since the goods now in process are those that were started up t years ago and at every instant since, the total value of labor tied up in the capital stock is
>
> $$\int_0^p Nw\frac{t}{p}dt = \frac{Nwp}{2}$$
>
> Thus the quantity of labor invested in the capital stock at any time is precisely half the value that is invested in the total output of a period of production. We may then write for the value of the capital stock
>
> $$K = \frac{Nwp}{2}$$
>
> (Dorfman, 1959a: 154; see also Lewin, 2011: 73–92)

K can then be inserted in the usual production function $Q = f(K, L)$, where Q is aggregate output and K and L are aggregate quantities of capital and labor respectively, and put through its usual paces.

Based on what we have already discussed, K as a measure of the aggregate value of the capital stock is totally incompatible with the subjective value approach to capital theory that we have in this Element regarded as fully Austrian and is (ironically) much more compatible with a Ricardian cost of production approach. In point of fact, for this reason it has been the object of devastating criticism even within the neoclassical literature.

8.2 Problems with the Aggregate Production Function

The criticism of the aggregate production function involves the claim that it relies on a fundamentally flawed general aggregation logic, notwithstanding its continued widespread use in theoretical and empirical studies in the neoclassical genre. Just how problematic this is has been known for decades because of the immanent criticism of Franklin Fisher and his collaborators (see Fisher [1993]; see Felipe & Fisher [2006] for the most recent review). A summary must suffice here to give the flavor of the overall critique (Fisher, 2005: 489).

Imagine that a production process can be characterized by a function of the form

$$q = f(k, l) \tag{2}$$

where q is output and k and l are the factors of production – knowing the values of the *quantities* of k and l one can accurately predict the *quantity* of q that will be produced. Imagine further that there are φ firms such that

$$q_z = f(\mathbf{k}_z, \mathbf{l}_z); z = 1 \ldots \varphi, ;$$
$$\mathbf{k} = k_i, (i = 1 \ldots n) \text{ and } \mathbf{l} = l_j, (j = 1 \ldots m). \tag{3}$$

$\mathbf{k}_z$ and $\mathbf{l}_z$ are *vectors* of different types of production goods and labor used in the z firms. Finally, consider the function

$$Q = F(K, L) \tag{4}$$

Q, K, and L are composites (aggregates) purportedly measuring the *quantity* of production, *quantity* of capital employed and *quantity* of labor employed.[31] There are φ consumption goods, n types of production good, and m types of labor services. Fisher et al. consider the following questions.

1. Under what conditions does equation 2 make sense? These are not trivial conditions. Clearly, k and l must be homogeneous identifiable entities whose services can be measured per period of time. The technical conditions must be known and, of the options available to combine them, the decision-maker is assumed consistently to choose the "correct" one. If, by contrast, k and l are heterogeneous collections, an aggregation problem exists *even at this firm or project level*. Further, if more than one output is jointly produced there is a problem of aggregating outputs.

2. How does one get from equation 3 to equation 4? This is the better known question of the two. Fisher et al. answer in no uncertain terms: except under the most unusual of circumstances, one *cannot*. And this applies *whether or not one assumes the economic system is in macroequilibrium*.

---

[31] More accurately, it is the *services* of capital and labor that are the inputs into production. K and L are stocks that when employed yield a flow of services per period of time.

Even ruling out the problem of within firm aggregation by assuming well-behaved production functions at the level of the firm, with comprehensive categories of homogeneous inputs, the conditions for successful across-firm aggregation are vanishingly likely to be met. First, there must be a state of *perpetual* long-run equilibrium. Second, if not in equilibrium, there must be *universal* constant returns to scale. Third, "even under constant returns to scale, the conditions for aggregation are so stringent as to make the existence of aggregate production functions in real economies a non-event. This is true not only for the existence of an aggregate capital stock but also for the existence of such constructs as aggregate labor or even aggregate output" (Fisher, 2005: 489).[32]

The last point raises the important question of why capital alone has been seen to be problematic in relation to the aggregation problem. The answer to this question goes to the very meaning of the concept of "capital" as used in economics.

Given these serious limitations of the aggregate production function as an empirically meaningful construct, what is one to make of the empirical studies that claim to find a "close fit" to the usual Cobb–Douglas form in the data on earnings for capital and labor? Fisher et al. find no validity in this instrumentalist defense of the aggregate production function as a close enough approximation.

Consider the aggregate accounting identity (available from aggregate data such as national accounting data):

$$Q = wL + rK \tag{5}$$

where Q is the value of final output (like GDP adjusted for inflation), L is the constant-price-index aggregate of labor, K is the constant-price-index aggregate of capital, w is the average wage of a unit of L, and r is the average rental rate of a unit of K. Totally differentiate this identity as follows.

$$d\log Q = \left(\tfrac{wL}{Q}\right) d\log L + \left(\tfrac{rK}{Q}\right) d\log K = \alpha\, d\log L + (1-\alpha) d\log K$$

where α is the *share* of L and $1-\alpha$ is the *share* of K, as the shares must add to 1. Integrating this equation gives

---

[32] Successful aggregation would mean that the aggregate production function that resulted behaved as the neoclassical theory says it should, with the input categories, such as K and L, providing unambiguous information about the variation of the components of these categories. K and L will behave like quantities of identifiable factors of production contributing marginal products (in terms of variations in the aggregate output) and for which there are the expected downward sloping demand curves. Realizing this, it is perhaps not surprising that aggregate production functions are never likely to be found in the real world.

$$Q = AL^a K^{1-a} \tag{6}$$

where A is the constant of integration. This looks like a Cobb–Douglass form (constant returns to scale). It should be emphasized, however, that $Q = AL^a K^{1-a}$ is *not* an approximation to $Q = wL + rK$; it is an *exact transformation*. Thus, it is not surprising that the Cobb–Douglas form of production function estimation gives a relatively good "fit" (see Felipe and McCombie [2014: 68–69] for more detailed discussion). The production function thus specified does not so much "explain" factor shares as express them in a different but equivalent way. A good fit does nothing to solve the heterogeneity problem or the ambiguities that attach to the categories of physically heterogeneous inputs and their earnings.

> While, over some restricted range of the data, approximations may appear to fit, good approximations to the true underlying technical relations require close approximation to the stringent aggregation conditions, and this is not a sensible thing to suppose. . . . When one works – as one must at an aggregate level – with quantities measured in value terms, the appearance of a well-behaved aggregate production function tells one nothing at all about whether there really is one. Such an appearance stems from the accounting identity that relates the value of outputs to the value of inputs – *nothing more*. (Fisher, 2005: 489)

The phrase "quantities measured in value terms" is noteworthy – this, indeed, is the root of all capital controversies. Consideration of the fundamentals underlying the capital concepts in current use, both from a Mengerian-Austrian perspective and from a critical neoclassical perspective, suggests many unresolved, and perhaps irresolvable, problems. Some theorists, such as Irving Fisher (1977) and Frank Fetter (1906), seem to have realized the problems and implicitly offered a solution by adopting a different approach to capital. As we have discussed, it was Ludwig von Mises, however, who focused on the role of capital in ordinary business life in facilitating decision-making through accounting and calculation (see Braun et al. [2016]). Capital as a financial value is a tool for coping with the undeniable bewildering heterogeneity of productive resources. It is what enables us to make decisions despite the multispecificity of most capital goods. What would a consistent theory of capital that incorporated this heterogeneity together with modern financial theory look like? This is the subject of the next section.

9 Capital in a Simple Financial Framework

9.1 John Hicks's Neo-Austrian Capital Framework

John Hicks has written extensively on capital. In addition to his three very influential books that have capital in their titles (1939, 1965, 1973), he has published numerous articles on capital theory. He was a scholar who returned many times in his life to the same questions, sometimes with different answers.[33] In *Value and Capital* (1939, second edition 1946) he critically considered Böhm-Bawerk's average period of production. His *Capital and Growth* (1965) was a series of exercises in growth theory. But, as with all of Hicks's work, this book contains much discussion of an informal nature. These extended discussions show that he was thinking carefully about the implications of time for the theory of capital. In a series of contributions in the 1970s, including his book *Capital and Time* (1973, also 1976, 1979 and 1979a), he became very concerned with time as a topic in economics. Along with this concern came a revived interest in the Austrian theory of capital (see Lewin [1997], on which we draw for much of the material in this section).

Hicks called his new approach to capital a *neo-Austrian* approach. In this section we begin by examining this framework and show how it fits together nicely with some concepts from the financial literature that has formed the basis of our treatment of capital in this Element.

Hicks begins with the importance of the "irreversibility of time." Time is not strictly analogous to space.

> One cannot escape the fact that the future is not determined in the same way as the past is. "How easy it is [however] to forget, when we contemplate the past, that much of what is now past was then future". This has profound implications for the meaning of any time series. "Action is always directed towards the future; but past actions when we contemplate them in their places in the stream of past events, lose their orientation toward the future which they undoubtedly possessed at the time when they were taken. We arrange past data in time-series, but our time series are not fully in time. The relation of year 9 to year 10 looks like it's relation to year 8; but in year 9 year 10 was future while year 8 was past. The actions of year 9 were based, or could be based, upon knowledge of year 8; but not on knowledge of year 10, only on guesses about year 10. For in year 9 the knowledge that we have about year 10 *did not yet exist.* (1976: 264, italics added)

One of the far-reaching implications of this concerns the theory of capital. Consider changes in the *value* of the capital stock.

> The value that is set upon the opening stock depends in part upon the value which is expected, at the beginning of the year, for the closing stock; but that was then the future, while at the end of the year it is already present (or past).

---

[33] "Capital (I am not the first to discover) is a very large subject, with many aspects; wherever one starts, it is hard to bring more than a few of them into view. It is just as if one were making pictures of a building; though it is the same building, it looks quite different from different angles. As I now realize, I have been walking round my subject, taking different views of it" (Hicks, 1973a: v).

There may be things which were included in the opening stock because, in *the light of information then available*, they seemed to be valuable; but at the end of the year it is clear that they are not valuable, so they have to be excluded. This may well mean that the net investment of year 1, calculated at the end of year 1, was over-valued – at least it seems to be over-valued from the standpoint of year 2. (1976: 265)

We examine the essentials of Hicks's conceptual framework (from *Capital and Time*) and attempt to draw out some of the implications and insights that emerge when interpreted from a subjectivist point of view. This framework is a convenient and efficient organizing device in which all of the various influences on the capital formation process come together.

9.2 A Simple Conceptual Framework

When we are dealing with production processes that use durable goods we are not able to impute the contribution of each input to particular outputs.

> Goods that are produced by the use of fixed capital are *jointly* supplied. It is the same capital good which is the source of the whole stream off outputs – outputs at different dates. . . . If it were not for the joint supply that is implied in the use of fixed capital, we could get on very well with the Böhm-Bawerkian model, in which we associated with every unit of final output a sequence of previous inputs which have "led to" that output; so that the cost of the final output is representable as a sum of the costs of the associated inputs, accumulated for each by interest for the appropriate length of time. In an economy which uses fixed capital such imputation is not possible. (Hicks, 1973a: 98–99)[34]

So Hicks agrees the "period of production" approach must be abandoned (though as we shall see later, it is Hicks himself who provided a "period of investment" approach that does much of what Böhm-Bawerk and Hayek asked of the APP and other more vague production period constructs). There is no measure of roundaboutness in purely physical terms.

---

[34] In a footnote to this Hicks notes: "The point, it may be remarked . . ., is well understood by the intelligent accountant. He is well aware that in the case of products that are jointly supplied, the allocation of overhead costs is arbitrary; and he is also aware that the depreciation allowances which he makes are arbitrary, for they similarly involve an allocation of common costs to the jointly produced outputs at different dates" (Hicks, 1973a: 99n). Compare our discussion in Section 5.3. Interestingly, Hicks does not say "optimal." Of course the implication is that the producer will choose the highest capital value from among the imagined alternatives (given any scale of operation). But, as we shall note, in the execution, in the unfolding of the plan, unexpected outcomes will cause the capital values to deviate from their planned contemplated levels. The continued viability of a plan thus depends on the considerations under discussion, whether or not it is considered optimal from some point of view. And the composition of the capital stock at any point of time will reflect the unfolding of these plans.

> What we must not abandon are Böhm-Bawerk's (and Menger's) true
> insights – the things that are the strength of the Austrian approach.
> Production is a process in time . . . . the characteristic form of production is
> a sequence, in which inputs are followed by outputs. Capital is an expression
> of sequential production. Production has a time structure so capital has a time
> structure. (Hicks, 1973a: 100)

To begin, we define a *production process* simply as a stream of inputs, giving
rise to a stream of outputs. A production process may be thought of also as a
technique (for converting inputs into outputs) or a *project*. It may take many
concrete forms, such as the building of a factory, or the construction of a
machine, or the exploration for oil, etc. followed by the flow of a particular
output (or set of outputs). Most production processes can be characterized in
this way. Inputs and outputs are to be thought of in terms of *value* (*or expected
value*), so outputs could be negative. Obviously, inputs must precede outputs at
the start of the project. It is important to emphasize that we calibrate the project
in value terms, even though, of course, we recognize the necessity of organizing combinations of physical quantities of diverse productive resources.

Hicks asks a fundamental motivating question: "What, in general, are the
conditions that must be satisfied in order that the process should be *viable*?"
(Hicks, 1973a: 100).

Considered in this way the question can be answered by the use of some
simple and familiar arithmetic which, though simple, has some important
implications. We start by looking at the situation faced by the *individual*
decision-maker ex ante. So the input and output values are *prospective*. In
this way we are attempting to uncover certain general principles that are
implicit in *any* production plan.

Every process (or project) has a capital value (familiar as the net present
value [NPV]). This is the discounted flow of the sum of the net values yielded
by the project over its life. Hicks shows that a necessary condition for the
viability of any process as a whole is that its capital value should be positive (or
at least nonnegative) *at every stage in its life* (Hicks, 1973b: 17; 1973a: 100). In
other words, the NPV should be positive whatever the date for which we make
the calculation. The capitalized value of the output flow must always be at least
as great as the capitalized value of the flow of inputs. If this were not the case
then the process should be abandoned at the point at which the NPV ceased to
be positive. At every stage in the life of the project the question of its
continuation may be raised. At each point this is essentially an investment
decision. So the project should not be continued if the value of what remains
(the remainder) at any date, and *as if contemplated from that date*, is not
positive (nonnegative). In other words, contemplated at the date of inception

it is possible to calculate a capital value at each imagined future date in the life of the project. Each and every such capital value, as contemplated by the decision-maker, must be nonnegative. If even one of them were negative that would indicate that the project should terminate at that date. In fact that defines the termination date.

While this general principle must be true as an implication of rational planning, as of the point in time of the decision, it may of course happen that *in the execution* (as distinct from the contemplation) of the project the capital value at some point before planned termination *unexpectedly* becomes negative – as it was originally conceived. This, obviously, does not imply that the project should be immediately abandoned (although in retrospect it would seem that it should not have been started). The principle of the irrelevance of sunk costs applies. It should be abandoned only if its capital value, *at that point in time*, is negative. Similarly the capital values at any point may during the execution of the project turn out to be unexpectedly high. Thus we may define a successful plan as one whose capital values turn out as expected (or better).

Of course present-value criteria are well known and are implied in all discussions of capital. What Hicks makes explicit here is the way in which present-value appraisals change over time, over the life of the project. He addresses the *intertemporal value structure* of a project, the logic within a single human plan concerning the relationship of the capital values at various contemplated dates to one another.

Hicks examines other ways of evaluating capital projects. Each plan (or capital project) will have an implicit yield, better known as the internal rate of return (IRR, yield). If the capitalization process is conducted using this rate then the initial value will be zero; it is the rate that causes the NPV at the inception date to be zero. If the same rate, the IRR, is used to calculate the capital values at all other dates, they will become positive, rise to a peak (or perhaps a series of peaks), and eventually fall again to zero at the termination point. Hicks also shows that for projects defined in this way the IRR is unique (Hicks, 1973b: 22, though this is true only for the particular way Hicks defines the start and end of any project). The foregoing can be greatly clarified with some basic algebra.

9.3 Formalization

Inputs and outputs. We denote *input* values and *output* values at time t (contemplated at time 0) as a_t and b_t. Also, $a_t = \sum_i w_{it} \alpha_{it}$, where w_{it} is the price and α_{it} is the quantity of input i at time t, assuming a set of ($i = 1, \ldots m$) inputs. For a multiproduct firm, $b_t = \sum_j p_{jt} \beta_{jt}$, where $j = 1, \ldots, \varphi$ is the set of outputs. For convenience we will suppress the i subscript, assuming only one type of input, and write $a_t = w_t \alpha_t$ without loss of generality (alternatively, preferably, α_t and w_t may be thought of as vectors). Similarly, we write $b_t = p_t \beta_t$, where p is the price and β the quantity of the output.

Net revenue – accounting profits. We define, $\pi_t = b_t - a_t$, as the *net output value* at any date t. This corresponds to what we normally think of as accounting profits, the difference between sales revenue and expenses, including, but not confined to, anticipated or *contractual* expenses for *wages, rental* of space and equipment, and also purchase of raw materials, advertising, etc. For durable capital goods – machines, buildings, tools – that are owned, a user cost must be imputed. The producer must treat these as if he were renting it to himself.[35] He purchases the services for these resources from himself. Normally, he will also have to pay *taxes* that must be subtracted from revenue or added to expenditures. Periodic interest payments on borrowed capital must be included in the calculation and subtracted from revenue to get net income (profit).

These profits, π, are paid to the owners or shareholders of the business and their level may be higher or lower than the level anticipated by them. In a neoclassical perfect equilibrium situation they will be zero. In a real-world dynamic competitive equilibrium they are the driving force of the market process. The entrepreneur is a profit seeker comparing the *rate* of profit earned with his expectations and with his estimate of alternative investment opportunities.

Capital-value (NPV or CV). We denote the *capital value at time t* by k_t.

$$k_t = \pi_t + \pi_{t+1}f + \pi_{t+2}f^2 + \ldots + \pi_n f^{(n-t)} = \sum_t^{n-t} \frac{\pi_t}{(1+r)^t} = \sum_t^{n-t} f^t \pi_t$$

$$(7)$$

where $f = 1/(1 + r)$, is the *discount factor* and r is the per period rate of interest, or more accurately, *rate of discount*. It is the present value of the (anticipated) flow of profits over the life of the project, n, commonly referred to as the discounted (net) cash flow. We may write it in the alternative form

$$k_t = \pi_t + fk_{t-1} = (b_t - a_t) + fk_{t-1} \qquad (7')$$

This says that the capital value at the *beginning* of any subperiod t, k_t, which is the discounted value of all of the remaining net (profits) outputs, can also be calculated as the net value of the profit of that period ($\pi_t = b_t - a_t$) plus the

---

[35] Refer to the discussion in Section 5.3 concerning capital maintenance.

capital value of the *remainder* for subperiods after t, fk_{t+1}. And this holds for any value of t.

Hicks now offers what he calls the "Fundamental Theorem": *it is always true that a fall in the rate of interest (rate of discount) will raise the capital value of any project throughout (that is as calculated at any date t), while a rise will lower it.* The proof follows from equation (7') and it is instructive to reproduce it here at some length.

> [S]uppose that the π's are unchanged but that r falls, so that the discount factor, [f,] rises. We see at once ... that k_t is bound to rise, provided that k_{t+1} is positive; and provided that k_{t+1} is not reduced by the fall in interest. But a similar argument applies to k_{t+1}. Thus we may go on repeating, up to the end of the process, where $k_n = \pi_n$. Thus k_n is unaffected by the fall in d; so k_{n-1} must be raised, and therefore k_{n-2} must be raised; and so on, back to k_t. So long as all the k_t's are positive (as we have seen that they must be, in order that the process should be viable), every k_t (0 to $n-1$) must be raised by the fall in the rate of interest.
>
> ... We have taken it for granted that the duration of the process remains at ($n+1$) weeks [subperiods], even though the rate of interest falls. But it is immediately clear that even if the duration is variable, it cannot be shortened. For since we have shown that with unchanged duration, every k_t ($t < n$) will be *raised*, it must still be advantageous to go on for at least the same duration, at a lower rate of interest. All that is possible is that the process may be lengthened.
>
> But the process will only be lengthened if k_{n+1} (which was zero at the higher rate of interest [discount]) becomes positive at the lower rate. That can happen, if the lengthening requires some net input (repairs, for instance, which become profitable only when the rate of interest falls). If it happens, however, all earlier k_t must be raised, a fortiori. So the Theorem continues to hold when duration is variable (Hicks, 1973a: 20–21).

This characterization of the investment plan thus shows, in the first instance, how the planner's appraisal will be affected by changes in the discount rate he applies. But it is equally clear that this appraisal will depend on all of the other conditions that characterize the project. For example, if the prices of the inputs w_t were to rise (or be expected to rise) the capital values would fall. Similarly a rise (expected rise) in the price of the product would raise all k_t. Changes in technology may affect these prices, by affecting processes elsewhere in the economy, or they may change the pattern of inputs, a_t, required.

The internal rate of return. The value of r for which $k_0 = 0$ is the internal rate of return (IRR). This can be thought of as the yield of the project. It represents the minimum that would have to be earned on any alternative project if this one were to be abandoned in its favor.[36] If "wages" w_t were to rise (uniformly) all of the k_t would be reduced. This implies that the yield of the project, its IRR, would fall. Thus for a given project (or set of projects) there is a trade-off between changes in w and d, other things constant. This is the sense in which the neo-Ricardians perceive the existence of a "factor price frontier" defining different equilibrium distributions of income between the factors of production. Considering hypothetical changes in w and changes in r necessary to "compensate" for these changes (by keeping $k_0 = 0$), one can imagine situations in which one technique, while dominant at a given level of r, loses its dominance as r falls and then regains it again as r continues to fall with rises in w. The significance of this hypothetical trade-off is far from clear, however, given that any pattern of inputs a_t is, in principle, possible. Also, there is no unambiguous way in which we can decide which project, or technique, is more "capital intensive" in the usual neoclassical sense of that term. This is discussed in more detail in the Appendix.

Moreover, it is important to note that in the context we have developed in the foregoing, r, or any measure of "interest," *cannot be taken to be the price or rate of earnings (profits) of capital.* r is the rate of discount applied to the overall earnings of the project at different dates. In fact the identification of w as "wages" includes payments for rentals of the services of physical production goods (as explained earlier) as well as for labor. The a_t inputs are "all inclusive." The "prices" or the "earnings" of capital goods are their "wages" understood in this way. This runs counter to the assumptions of the neo-Ricardians, who identify "interest" as the earnings of capital.

9.4 Looking Forward and Looking Backward

It should be emphasized that this view of the production process presented in the foregoing is a forward-looking one. All of the values are prospective. As such there is an unavoidable, but often suppressed speculative element to it. There is at least one other possible way to look at capital processes in time, that is, *retrospectively*, as a *result* of *capital invested*. From equation (7′),

---

[36] The use of an IRR is a matter of financial convention. It depends not only on how one divides up a project over time, but also on assuming that the "internal" yield is the same for each subperiod. It seems intuitively clear, however, that the individual planner must have in mind some benchmark against which to (subjectively) test the attractiveness of a project in comparison, for example, with investing in the market. Each planner will define his own boundaries. Also, it is well-known that NPV is considered to be superior to IRR as a criterion by which to compare possible investments. In some rare instances they may give different rankings. We assume the individual planner will use the criterion most preferred.

$$k_0 = \pi_0 + f\,\pi_1 + f^2\pi_2 + \ldots \quad + f^{(t-1)}\pi_{t-1} + f^t k_t \tag{8}$$

for any value t between 0 and n. Using the IRR in f, $k_0 = 0$, so,

$$k_t = (-\pi_0)(f)^{-t} + (-\pi_1)(f)^{-(t-1)} + \ldots \quad + (-\pi_{t-1})(f)^{-1} \tag{8'}$$

Looked at it this way, k_t is the sum of the net inputs, $-\pi = a - b$, from 0 to $t - 1$, *accumulated* by interest up to week t. This captures the idea of inputs maturing at a rate equal to the IRR and emerging as a final output.

For plans that are successful, in the sense that the capital values k_t turn out to be exactly equal to what they were expected to be, when *discounted or accumulated* using the IRR, it should be clear that the two ways of looking at capital (prospective and retrospective) are exactly equivalent; they describe an ongoing and, in an essential sense, unchanging process. This is what the assumption of a steady state buys us, namely that the process, all processes, look the same at all points of time and *for* all points of time. In the steady state, as all plans are successful in this sense, the interest rate on loans must be equal to the (known) yield on projects, and the latter must be uniform (for any given investment period) across projects. We are in a Ricardian world.

Hicks is critical of the steady state: "I am very skeptical of the importance of such 'steady state' theory. The real world (perhaps fortunately) is not, and never is, in a steady state .... A 'steady state' theory is out of time; but an Austrian theory is in time" (Hicks, 1973a: 109). And he goes on to explain that a theory that is in time would have to take note of history, would have to include inherited history, including the inevitably less than optimal capital stock, as a "cause" of subsequent events. For a theory that is in time, perspective matters, things look very different from different points of time. Any process with a yield that is greater than the market rate of interest on loans, or any other appropriate opportunity cost, would have the property that *the capital-value measured forward (prospectively) will be greater than the backward (retrospective) measure*. And this will be true even at point 0 where $k_0 = 0$ measured forward. This is a basic implication of rational planning. If a process is successfully being carried out, and if its yield is greater than the interest rate, a *capital gain will accrue at each stage of the process*. The existence of profit, in this sense, absolutely depends on a disequilibrium between the yield and the interest rate. And this can persist only if there is no steady state, if there is no uniform (zero by this definition) rate of profit. The existence of profits implies different (varying) expectations.

Technical progress will imply that the yield on new processes (embodying the new knowledge) will be above that on old processes (those processes that do not).

Old processes will, if there is enough time, be replaced by new ones. The capital stock, the stock of tangible things, will, at any point of time, reflect the accumulated results of passed gains in knowledge. Although this is inimical to the steady state, everything that has been said above with regard to the characterization of projects, techniques, and processes that make up capital remains valid.

Social accounting, however, can be done consistently only in a steady state. Out of the steady state (a limiting case of which is the Ricardian stationary state) it is strictly impossible to derive aggregate values for capital and therefore for output (since the value of output depends on the value attributed to capital maintenance). Hicks explains this, yet then proceeds to assume a steady state in order to explore aspects of social accounting and transitions between such states, a path along which we shall not follow. Nevertheless his simple arithmetic framework reveals a lot for those who believe that the market process should be analyzed as a disequilibrium phenomenon.

9.5 Capital Plans and Macroeconomics

Hicks's framework in the form presented in the foregoing is a convenient way to think about capital. It is fully consistent with the Austrian approach including those developed by Hayek, Lachmann, and Kirzner. According to this approach capital must be thought of in terms of intertemporal plans. We must make a distinction between capital goods and capital as an abstract category. The latter refers to the *value* to be attributed to a particular plan or set of production plans. The profits or losses to be attributed to a production plan are the result of changes (or the absence thereof) in the capital values attributed to it over time. These appreciations (or deprecations) in value are, in turn, the result of (are derived from) changes in consumers' evaluation of final production.

The meaning and the value of any particular capital good derives from its position in a particular production plan. "The identification of a 'resource' as distinct from other physical things, cannot be made without reference to human purposes (Kirzner, 1966: 38). All capital goods are, in effect, an expression of "unfinished plans" (Kirzner, 1966, chapter 1). As such, these capital goods can be valued by what they add to the value of the plan.

The value of any income source is derived from the income it is expected to produce; so the value of any single capital good is familiarly thought of as being equal to the discounted value of the estimated income it adds to any production plan – the discounted value of its marginal product.

All production plans are affected by, among other things, changes in the rate of discount that is pertinent to the plan. A fall in the discount rate will increase its value, a rise will decrease it. Thus if rates of discount are affected generally by macroeconomic changes, notably changes in interest rates, these may be expected to have a general effect on the expected value of existing and planned capital projects. In particular, those projects with the longest time horizon will be most affected. (This is well known and expressed in the proposition that the elasticity of present value is higher the higher the time horizon.) Certain familiar macroeconomic scenarios thus follow from any general change in rates of discount that follow upon general changes in interest rates and (more importantly) *expected* interest rates. Thus, for example, producers perceiving a fall in the "social" rate of time preference (as translated in market rates of interest) will be led to the adoption of plans with longer time horizons, as suggested by the Austrian theory of the business cycle. As explained, however, it is important to remember that the discount rate is only one of the variables that affects the capital values of any and all projects. Hicks's approach has the virtue of providing us with a particularly clear framework in which the various influences may be revealed. So we might write a general capital value (vector) function as

$$k_t = k_t(w, \alpha, \ p, \beta, \ r),$$

indicating that r, the money interest rate (or interest rate structure) is only one of the determinants of k_t. r is perhaps especially important because of its macroeconomic significance as the indicator of the relationship between present and future prices of consumption goods. However, the structure of prices and wages in general may affect the project (through p and w) and technology obviously matters (α and β). Our framework gives a comprehensive picture that might be useful for future research. It is also a framework that is consistent with the EVA® framework from modern financial practice, used recently in connection with ABCT. See the mathematical note that follows.

Mathematical Note: The EVA® Framework

Two key concepts of the EVA® framework are economic value added (EVA) and market value added (MVA).

EVA is the economic value added in period t, equal to what we have called profit, π_t.

$$\pi_t = \text{EVA}_t$$

MVA, is the present value of all future EVAs

$$\text{MVA} = \sum_{t=1}^{\infty} \frac{\text{EVA}_t}{(1+r)^t} = \sum_{t=1}^{\infty} \frac{\pi_t}{(1+r)^t}$$

Therefore, the capital value at time 0 equals the spot market value plus the expected MVA:

$$k_0 = K_0 + \text{MVA}$$

where K_0 is the money value of the investment in period 0 (the financing phase).

See Figure 1 in Section 1.2. The production process is there depicted as proceeding from an initial investment of K_0 adding value over n periods to a final accumulated value of K_n, the present value of which is k_0 (valued at time 0, contemplating all of the earnings of the project).

A fall in the discount rate will affect k_0 by affecting MVA, the extent of which depends on the interest elasticity of this present value, a concept we analyze in the next section (see Cachanosky & Lewin, 2014, 2016a, 2016b, 2018; Lewin & Cachanosky, 2016, 2018a, 2018b).

9.6 Considering the Austrian Business Cycle: Discount Rates Changes and Time

We have shown that the development of ACT was strongly influenced by the desire to use Böhm-Bawerk's simple APP to illustrate the nature of money–credit-induced business cycles, the approach we now call ABCT. Summarizing briefly, Böhm-Bawerk tried to capture in *quantitative* terms *the average amount of time taken in any production project – a purely physical measure of physical capital.* Except for the most simple of cases, this is impossible. As soon as one considers the relationship between capital and time, *value* enters the analysis and a purely physical (quantitative) measure is impossible. We show now that Böhm-Bawerk's essential error lies not in his attempt to take account of time considerations in the mind of the investor/entrepreneur as expressed in some simple formulation, but, rather, in his attempt to do so by confining his attention to a *strictly ph*ysical measure. As John Hicks had already pointed out as early as 1939 (1939, 186) a valid form of the APP *does* exist – he called it the *average period* (AP). It is exactly that same construct developed by Frederick Macaulay[37] in 1938 (Macaulay, 1938), known as "duration." Duration (D) is most easily understood as *the average amount of time for which one has to wait for 1* in any investment. It is a measure of the "length" of the project – or, at least, some significant aspect of the length. It captures an important aspect of what is in the investor's mind as he contemplates his investment.

Specifically,

---

[37] See also Lewin and Cachanosky (2014).

Table 3 APP and *AP*

Böhm-Bawerk's APP – labor input weights	Hicks's AP (Macaulay's *D*) – present value (output) weights

$$\sum_{t}^{n-t}\left\{ \underbrace{\frac{l_t}{\underbrace{\sum_{t}^{n-t}l_t}_{\text{weight}}}}\cdot\underbrace{(n-t)}_{\text{time}} \right\} \qquad \sum_{t}^{n-t}\left\{ \underbrace{\frac{f^t\pi_t}{\underbrace{\sum_{t}^{n-t}f^t\pi_t}_{\text{weight}}}}\cdot\underbrace{(t)}_{\text{time}} \right\}$$

$$\text{AP} = D_t = \sum_{t}^{n-t}\left(\frac{f^t\pi_t}{\sum_{t}^{n-t}f\pi_t}\right)(t) = \sum_{t}^{n-t}\left(\frac{f^t\pi_t}{k_t}\right)(t) \tag{9}$$

where the terms are as previously defined, remembering that $f = 1/(1 + r)$.[38] Note AP is a weighted average of the number of *time units* involved in the project, starting from t, the current point of observation, to n, the last, where the weights are the *proportions of total the present value of the value added in the time period* $(f^t\pi_t/k_t)$. It is the (present) value-weighted amount of time involved in the investment. As such it is a *money value of time* measure.

A comparison with Böhm-Bawerk's APP is very revealing. See Table 3.

The difference between the two time indexes, $n - t$ for Böhm-Bawerk, and t for Hicks, indicates that the former uses *input* weights and the latter uses *output* weights.

The logic is simple. The economic significance of the time involved in the investment, the amount of time for which one has to wait for earnings, is dependent on the relative size of net receipts in each of the periods. The simple size of the calendar time, n (at time t_0), is not very informative. The same n can have very different significance to the investor depending on whether the payments occur sooner or later and in what proportions. The value significance of the time involved must be considered. Given time preference, other things constant, a longer average period (duration) should carry a higher markup. These are the essentials of the *money value of time* (*the other side of the time value of money*). The amount of time involved in any investment is valued according to the influence of value on time.

---

[38] We make the usual assumption that the rate of discount applied in each period d_t is the same for all periods.

9.7 *D* as a Measure of the Interest Elasticity of the Capital Value of the Investment

Using equation 7 to characterize investments (where r is presumed equal for all subperiods), the sensitivity of the k_t to changes in interest rates (more specifically to the rate of discount applied to the investment) is a key factor in investment appraisal. And financial specialists have long worked to develop tools to mitigate, if not completely *immunize*, investments from this risk.

It is well known in the financial literature that D has a different and additional use from the one of measuring the time intensity of the invested dollars, namely as a measure of *the interest elasticity of NPV (or CV)*, k, of the investment. This dual aspect of D is significant.

Hicks (1939) already indicated that D ($=AP$) is also a measure of *the elasticity of the (present) value of the project with respect to the discount f*. It measures how any estimate of net present value changes with a change in the discount factor, for small changes.

Hicks's formulation (1939, 186) proceeds as follows: The capital value (NPV) of any stream of n payments (cash-flows) is given as before by

$$k_t = \sum_t^{n-t} \frac{\pi_t}{(1+r)^{n-t}} = \sum_t^{n-t} f^t \pi_t \tag{7}$$

We may calculate the *elasticity* of k_t with respect to f as

$$E_{k_t f} = \frac{E(k_t)}{E(f)} = \frac{1}{k_t} [tf^t \pi_t + (t+1)f^{t+1}\pi_{t+1} + \ldots \quad + nf^n \pi_n] = \sum_t^{n-t} (t) \left(\frac{f^t \pi_t}{k_t} \right)$$

where E is the elasticity (or d log) operator. This follows from the rule that the elasticity of a sum is the weighted average of the elasticities of its parts.[39]

To repeat, E_{kf} is revealed to have two uses. First, as just shown, it is a measure of the sensitivity of the value of the project (investment) to changes in the rate of discount, or (inversely) in the discount factor. So, anything that affects the discount rate applied to investments will affect their *relative valuations*. Significantly, the perceived values of investment projects that constitute the components of the capital structure of an economy will be unevenly

---

[39] This may be seen more clearly if we consider the case of k_0, the capital value of an n period investment evaluated at point 0. $k_0 = \sum_{t=0}^n \frac{\pi_t}{(1+r)^t} = \sum_{t=0}^n f^t \pi_t$. Calculating the *elasticity* of k_0 with respect to f: $E_{k_0 f} = \frac{E(k_0)}{E(f)} = \frac{1}{k_0} [\pi_0 + f^1 \pi_1 + 2f^2 \pi_2 + 3f^3 \pi_3 \pi + nf^n \pi_n] = \sum_{t=0}^n (t) \left(\frac{f^t \pi_t}{k_t} \right)$ which is D ($=AP$) evaluated at point 0. The case considered in the text is k_t the capital-value of an investment going from point t to point n evaluated at point t. So it has a total of $n - t$ time periods. This makes for ease of comparison with Böhm-Bawerk's APP and also fits with Hicks's formulation that is able to consider a separate capital value as evaluated at each point of time, t.

affected by monetary policy that systematically affects discount rates. Those components of existing production processes that have a higher $E_{k,f}$ will be relatively more affected – for example, a fall in the discount rate (perhaps provoked by a fall in the federal funds and other interest rates) will produce a rise in the value of high-$E_{k,f}$ projects relative to those with lower ones.

$E_{k,f}$ (Hicks's AP) is also Macaulay's duration.[40] D thus serves the dual purpose of measuring both "roundaboutness" and the sensitivity of capital value to changes in the discount rate (factor). The two aspects of D may be seen as a time weighted average of proportional responses in k_t and as a value weighted average of the time involved in any investment, respectively. It is the same formula with different components respectively being considered to be weights for summing the other components.

It is only in the second aspect – as a measure of response, as first formulated by Macaulay and subsequently further developed, that has been of interest to the finance discipline, but both are of interest to economists and have wider application for them.[41]

10 Conclusion: The Entrepreneur Adds Value by Capitalizing Resources

In this Element we have attempted to outline the elements essential for understanding Austrian Capital Theory (ACT). A good grasp of ACT is absolutely necessary for understanding what Austrian economics is all about, and how it differs from the mainstream and other heterodox schools of economics, both in its reasoning and in its policy implications.

If one were to pick the one theoretical component that distinguishes Austrian from mainstream economics, it would surely have to be the presence of the entrepreneur. Neoclassical economic analysis has almost nothing to say about the entrepreneur. Its equilibrium analysis proceeds in terms of the eradication of all profit opportunities, and, if there are no profits there will be no entrepreneurs. More accurately, the entrepreneur is that shadowy figure who ensures

---

[40] " . . . when we look at the form of this elasticity we see that it may be very properly described as the *Average Period [AP]* of the stream [of earnings]; for it is the *average length of time for which the various payments are deferred from the present, when the times of deferment are weighted by the discounted values of the payments*" (Hicks, 1939: 186, italics in original; see also 218–222).

[41] For the development of and the forms and uses of *duration* in different situations that may be of use to Austrian researchers a number of useful surveys exist, including Bierwag et al. (1983) and Bierwag and Fooladi (2006). One variation known as *modified duration* measures the elasticity of present value with respect to changes in the discount *rate* (rather than the discount *factor*) and might be of more immediate use in discussions of ABCT. Also for real-world discrete (as opposed to small theoretical) changes D cannot be taken as constant as the discount rate varies (a phenomenon known as *convexity*) and various corrections exist to deal with this. For a comprehensive, if challenging, treatment see Osbourne (2005, 2014).

that profits cannot last for very long in the theory. His appearance is instanta-
neously eradicated en route to the final equilibrium that is the center of the
analysis. By contrast, the entrepreneur is the heart and soul of Austrian
economics, wherein he is a vibrant, busy, creative, reckless, innovator. He is
a prominent, perpetual presence. As Mises and Kirzner affirm, he is the driving
force of the market process. For Austrians, economics without the entrepreneur
is like the proverbial *Hamlet* without the prince. If the objective is to understand
the how real-world markets work, the entrepreneur must take center stage.

We share Ludwig Lachmann's view of the entrepreneur. He is the organizer,
assembler, of capital combinations (productive resources – human and physical). In pursuit of profit, motivated by his own, perhaps unique, vision of what
is achievable, he brings together complementary components of a production
plan. The plan is adaptable and some of these components may have to be
substituted for others, or scrapped, in light of unexpected occurrences. In this
way the planned complementarity of the entrepreneur becomes part of the
spontaneous complementarity of the market of entrepreneurs.

Crucially, the entrepreneur's production plan must be informed also by the
ability of the entrepreneur to calibrate its ongoing performance in terms of
money, using the methods and conventions of capital accounting and the
financing facilities of capital markets which have their own conventions.
Thus we share also Ludwig von Mises's view of the entrepreneur as a calculator, estimator, decision-maker extraordinaire in the production process. One
must distinguish carefully between capital goods and capital, the latter being a
necessary concept unique to private property, profit-and-loss economies.
"Capital" is the result of "capitalizing" the revenue stream, the *value added*,
from successful production. In this Element we have tried to draw out some of
the details of this capitalization process in the hope that it may be of some use in
ongoing applications involving ACT.

As in most things Austrian, Carl Menger's work informs all aspects of our
view on capital including the importance of time in production (Böhm-Bawerk
and Hayek) as well as the importance of monetary calculation (Mises). The
Austrian theorists focusing on "time in production" have tended to emphasize
the "physical" dimension of capital. In this essay we have suggested a reor-
ientation toward the "value" dimension.

In brief, the entrepreneur creates value for the consumer by using (deploy-
ing) capital to assemble productive resources in complementary combinations
over time. This, we believe, is the nature of capital, and the essence of
capitalism, and in this the diverse views of the Austrians who have worked
on it come together in a unified view of ACT.

Appendix
The Neo-Ricardian Challenge and Its Misconceptions

A.1 Background

In the traditional neoclassical economics framework, that is widely taken for granted by most finance and economics scholars, capital and labor are considered to be categories of productive resources that are combined in production to add value. The prices of the services of the various kinds of labor and capital-goods employed in production are presumed to be determined by the marginal additions of these services to the revenue of the productive firm – their marginal value products. There is a compelling logic of choice involved. If, in the judgement of the employer/entrepreneur, the additional value of the labor or capital good's service is not at least equal to the estimated addition to revenue, it will not be purchased – the factors will not be employed. In this way, individual earnings, of workers or owners of capital goods are determined by their functions in production. It is a functional account of the distribution of earnings.

There is an historical, but ongoing, challenge to the very concept of capital as a factor of production that earns a marginal product. Consideration of the relationship between capital value and the discount rate is the key factor in this challenge. The validity of the functional distribution of earnings is denied in favor of an explanation based on the spending propensities and power, of the various "social classes" (deriving from the work of the classical economist David Ricardo). This challenge is the essence of the so-called "Cambridge capital controversy" between MIT (Cambridge, MA, USA) and Cambridge University (UK) during the 1960s and 1970s.[1]

In support of their case, the UK neo-Ricardians mounted an attack on neoclassical production theory based on the identification of certain theoretical "paradoxes." These paradoxes consist of cases in which it is alleged, for example, that a fall in the interest rate (equated to the "rate of profit" earned by "capital"), which, according to neoclassical production theory is expected to bring about an increase in the demand for capital in production, can lead to the exact opposite at some interest rates. More specifically, a fall in the interest rate may first lead to the adoption a more "capital-intensive" productive technique, and then switch, paradoxically, to a less "capital-intensive" technique, and then

---

[1] For a recap of the debate see Cohen and Harcourt (2003) and the references therein.

switch back again as the interest rate continues to fall. These are alternative techniques, characterized by their *physical* capital labor ratios. In other words, switches may occur, as well as reswitches and reversals (moving among three or more techniques in paradoxical fashion). In short, *there is no monotonic relationship between capital and the rate of interest.* This means that as long as interest rate is considered the price of capital, then there is no well-behaved demand function of capital. This would be a serious pitfall in the core of the neoclassical production theory.

To avoid misinterpretation, it is very important to emphasize that the neo-Ricardian framework (though perhaps not the intent of its critique) is strictly comparative statics. There is no analysis of real-time changes in interest rates and related changes in production. Rather their analysis involves comparing alternative equilibrium (steady-state) situations. It is not clear if any insights gained from comparative statics can be applied to real world comparative disequilibrium situations, unless an "as if" methodology is adopted and used to make empirical generalizations. This, however, does not appear to be their strategy.

Nevertheless, these anomalies are taken to be devastating to the entire neoclassical edifice, based as it is on a quantity of capital earning a marginal product. The whole notion of a production-function is rendered meaningless by their account. Though the neoclassicals (Cambridge, MA, USA) conceded the logic of the neo-Ricardian (Cambridge, UK) attack, they doubted its relevance and have continued to use the neoclassical framework undeterred. The neo-Ricardians thus continue to attack, to this day, indignant at the intransigence of the neoclassicals in refusing to abandon the neoclassical framework and refusing to embrace the neo-Ricardian alternative in its place (see Lewin & Cachanosky, 2018b).

It is not possible, nor relevant, to examine here the details of this episode or its ongoing developments.[2] Our interest is solely in the light that it sheds on notions of capital, and, especially on the relationship between capital and time. For that purpose it will be illustrative to analyze certain aspects of the so-called paradoxes.

---

[2] It is our conviction that the assertions of the neo-Ricardians were decisively debunked by Yeager (1976) – who clarified the source of the so-called paradoxes and provided an alternative perspective for understanding the nature of capital and its earnings, in which no such paradoxes appear. In effect, Yeager shows that the entire case of the neo-Ricardians is based on a fundamental category mistake in regards to what capital is and what it earns. We shall make use of this in what follows. In a more recent contribution, Garrison (2006) returns to Yeager's analysis in order to explain why the neo-Ricardians summarily dismissed Yeager's argument without even considering it. We shall make use of this too.

A.2 A Simple Illustrative Example

To do this we borrow the example used by Garrison (2006: 190–196). This example is similar to the one used by Yeager (1976), which he in turn adopted from a seminal article by Samuelson (1966). In examples of this kind, the neo-Ricardians refer to a "technique" of production as a method of producing a particular output of a given product with given amounts of labor input in specific periods. *Any nonlabor inputs are implicit in the analysis.* The techniques are fixed, and the output they produce is fixed as well as the prices of the inputs and the output. Two such techniques are given in Table A.1.

The two techniques are distinguished mainly by the *timing* of their (original) labor inputs (units of labor-service), and only minimally by the *amount* of labor required. Technique B is identified as the more "capital-intensive" because it requires less labor to produce the same output. "Capital intensity" is a purely physical matter.[3] If we now consider the cost of financing each technique we get a paradoxical result.

Imagine each unit of labor costs \$1; then the cost of financing each technique at a 5% interest rate is given in Table A.2.

The general expression is in Table A.2, where r is the rate-of-interest (discount) used to compound labor inputs. Note, although, for concreteness, we are using money values (dollars) to value the labor inputs by assuming each unit to be worth \$1, this assumption is unnecessary. The analysis applies whatever metric is used to value the labor inputs as long as it is constant. The analysis would work even if we used elementary labor units and count the

Table A.1 Labor requirement by technique

	Labor hours required	
Time period	**Technique A**	**Technique B**
1	100	
2		210
3	110.16	
Total	210.16	210

---

[3] The neo-Ricardians identify all "capital" as intermediate goods, such as machines, tools, or raw materials. They are goods-in-process from the original labor that constructed them, to the emergence of the final consumer good. So all capital goods (can be and) are reduced to dated labor. In this way, we get a *purely physical* measure of "capital," one that, by construction, does not vary with the interest rate.

Table A.2 Cost by technique (interest rate = 5%)

	Cost ($)	
Time period	Technique A	Technique B
1	100.00	205.88
2	105.00	210.00
3	220.41	220.50

Table A.2a Cost by technique for interest rate r

	Cost	
Time period	Technique A	Technique B
1	100.00	
2	$100.00(1 + d)$	210.00
3	$100(1 + d)^2 + 110.16$	$210(1 + d)$

interest rate as the mechanism by which such labor is augmented. Compare Hayek's triangle.

At 5% technique A is the cheaper to finance, and hence the one that will be chosen. But this is not true for all interest rates, as can be shown by repeating the process for various interest rates according to the information in Table A.2a. Techniques A and B can be described by the expressions $100(1 + d)^2 + 110.16$ and $210(1 + d)$, respectively. Calculating their NPVs at various interest rates yields Table A.3. The output produced by both techniques is identical and invariant and thus can be ignored in this analysis.

At interest rates below 2% technique B is adopted. Between interest rates of 2% and 8% technique A is adopted but a reswitch occurs at interest rates higher than 8%, where, paradoxically, the more "capital-intensive" technique B is chosen. See Figure A.1. This example reveals the essence of the neo-Ricardian case.

Another way to tell the story is to consider techniques A and B as aspects of a single decision, with the option not chosen seen as the opportunity cost of the decision. In this way we can combine the two configurations to yield the equation of the project, for the rate of return, d.

$$PV(A) - PV(B) = 100(1 + r)^2 - 210(1 + r) + 110.16 = 0$$

This is a second-order polynomial that has two roots (IRRs), $(1 + d) = 1.02$ and $(1 + r) = 1.08$, no paradox there.

Table A.3 NPV by technique

Interest rate (%)	Relative costs		
	NPV (A)	NPV (B)	NPV (A)/ NPV (B)
0	210.16	210	1.0008
1	212.17	212.1	1.0003
2	214.2	214.2	1.00000
3	216.25	216.3	0.99977
4	218.32	218.4	0.99963
5	220.41	220.5	0.99959
6	222.52	222.6	0.99964
7	224.65	224.7	0.99978
8	226.8	226.8	1.00000
9	228.97	228.9	1.00031
10	231.16	231	1.00069

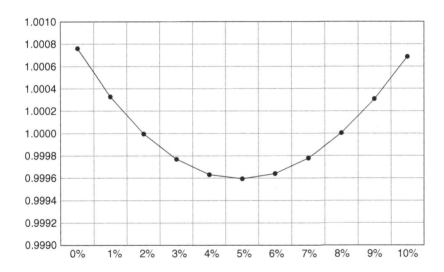

Figure A.1 NPV(A)/NPV(B) by discount rate.

A.3 Evaluation

In this stark form, and given the number of restrictive assumptions, including the lack of substitutability within techniques, and the invariance of all relative prices, it may seem as if the paradoxes identified are merely theoretical curiosities without much practical significance. This may be true. However, the discussion does raise interesting issues concerning categories.

The neo-Ricardian paradoxes occur because of their insistence that "capital," to be a useful category as a factor of production, must be physically measurable, on a par with physical labor. And what our discussion previously has shown is that a purely physical measure of capital is impossible. Indeed, this has been well known at least since pointed out by Wicksell ([1911] 1934). Any attempt to "count" the "amount" of capital units encounters the interest rate, which is a price that introduces value into the exercise and contaminates its pure physical-ness. Therefore, according to the neo-Ricardians, capital *should not be considered as a factor of production* exhibiting scarcity, having a price and a demand curve. And this is so much the worse for all neoclassical constructs that depend on it, most notably the aggregate *production function* that is used to explain the earnings of "labor" and "capital."

The problems in this criticism are in its understanding of capital. Our previous discussion clearly suggests that capital, by its very nature, is a value construct. The collection of things that we, perhaps unfortunately, call *capital goods* do not constitute the economy's capital. Indeed, we agree *capital is not a factor of production*. Rather, capital refers to the *value* of any such collection (in terms of its potential to produce useful things). There is, moreover, no category difference between the *capital value* of labor employed and the capital value of the capital goods employed. The fact that capital goods can conceptually be traced back all the way to the input of "pure" labor (and nature) is entirely irrelevant for investment decisions in a market economy, which are, as are all such decisions, necessarily forward-looking. An investor contemplating the financing of any given project, for example, as described for techniques A and B considered earlier, cares only about the relative cost to him of each (or alternatively, the *PV* of their prospective profits, their relative *capital values*). Capital in this context refers to the accumulated value to be expected from the investment, or at any moment to the accumulated value up to that moment. There is no reason to expect "capital intensity" to be an invariant property of any technique. In terms of the amount of pure labor to nonlabor inputs the "capital intensity" of a technique will fluctuate with the interest rate as its capital value changes. There is no paradox.

Also important, the neo-Ricardians identify the price of capital as the *rate-of-interest* which they regard as synonymous with the rate of profit. But neither is correct. The market interest rate is, indeed, the price of capital as we understand it. It is the cost of borrowing "capital" for the employment of any valuable resource or for any other reason. It is the price of *credit* and is determined by the time preferences of borrowers and lenders and the production possibilities available. (The neo-Ricardians have no discussion of what determines interest rates.)

The interest rate is *not* the price paid for the services of *capital goods*, and it is *not* the rate of profit. The price of the services of capital goods is a rental rate on capital goods. It is well understood, for example, that a firm renting a copy machine pays a monthly fee for its services. If it owns the copy machine, sound accounting dictates that it must charge itself something like the rental rate for its services – which may be the basis of a depreciation fund. It is dimensionally equivalent to labor, conceived as *human capital.* Labor services cannot be alienated from their owner, so they must be rented. The rental rate on labor (human capital) is what we call wages. And profits are the residual value left over after interest and all factor costs (wages and the rents of capital goods) are paid. Profits are the reward for being right in an uncertain world.

Consider the example in Table A.1. If, instead of labor inputs, we imagine these to be the inputs of mechanical robots (not so fanciful in today's economy) that are rented by the firm. Then the rental paid for the services of any robot is its "wage." By the reckoning of the neo-Ricardians, both techniques have 100% capital intensity, or, more accurately, the capital intensity cannot be figured out until we know how much pure labor was used – or, since theirs is a strictly static equilibrium exercise – needs to be used to construct the robots. From the perspective of real-world investment decision-making, however, this is irrelevant.

So what is "capital intensity"? Considering that two projects (techniques, investments) with the same NPV may have different *durations, D's (AP's),* the one with the higher D may sensibly be considered to be more capital intensive. For two projects with the same D, the one with the higher NPV may sensibly be considered the more capital intensive (in the sense of embodying more financial capital). In each case the more capital intensive the project the more its capital value will be affected by a change in the discount rate. Capital intensity and interest rate sensitivity are two sides of the same coin. And capital intensity thus considered is not an invariant property of any project (see Cachanosky & Lewin, 2014).

The functional distribution of earnings remains intact. At any moment in time there exists a set of technical possibilities for the production of useful things. We can call these *production functions.* The inputs into these *production functions* are the physically homogeneous productive resources, of whatever kind, that are available. Because resources are very heterogeneous, capital goods more than labor, there will be very many categories of inputs. But for each kind, there will be a price and a demand-curve implicit from the *production function.* There is no reswitching in terms of physical inputs. To be sure, in a general equilibrium setting, factor prices may appear to act perversely, because of complicated complementary relationships in production, but this is hardly news. There is an elementary distinction between demand-curve shifts and movements along them.

The colloquial understanding of capital as *financial capital* is after all close to the mark, at least closer than thinking of capital as a collection of physical things. The latter is perhaps responsible for more confusion and controversy than clarity. A consideration of the role of time in production and investment decisions, as explored in this Element, brings one to the realization that capital is the result of a process of evaluation, of "capital accounting." The ability to use capital accounting in an important and necessary component of the phenomenal success of *capital*ism.

References

Bierwag, G., & Fooladi, I. (2006). Duration analysis: An historical perspective. *Journal of Applied Finance*, 16(2), 144–160.

Bierwag, G., Kaufman, G., & Toevs, A. (1983). Duration: Its development and use in bond portfolio management. *Financial Analysts Journal*, 39(4), 15–35.

Birner, J. (1999). The place of the Ricardo effect in Hayek's economic research programme. *Revue d'économie politique*, 109(6), 803–816.

Böhm-Bawerk, E. v. (1890). *Capital and Interest: A Critical History of Economical Theory*. (G. D. Senholz, trans.). South Holland, IL: Libertarian Press, 1959.

Bornier, J. M. (n.d.). Comparing Menger and Böhm-Bawerk on capital theory. Retrieved from http://junon.univ-cezanne.fr/bornier/lastp.html

Braun, E. (2015a). Carl Menger's contribution to capital theory. *History of Economic Ideas*, 23(1), 77–99.

Braun, E. (2015b). The theory of capital as a theory of capitalism – hidden Austrian contributions to a historically specific approach to capital. Retrieved from: https://ideas.repec.org/p/tuc/tucewp/0015.html

Braun, E. (2017). The theory of capital as a theory of capitalism. *Journal of Institutional Economics*, 13(2), 305–325.

Braun, E., Lewin, P., & Cachanosky, N. (2016). Ludwig Von Mises's approach to capital as a bridge between Austrian and institutional economics. *Journal of Institutional Economics*, doi:10.1017/S1744137416000102.

Cachanosky, N., & Lewin, P. (2014). Roundaboutness is not a mysterious concept: A financial application to capital theory. *Review of Political Economy*, 26(4), 648–665.

Cachanosky, N., & Lewin, P. (2016a). Financial foundations of Austrian business cycle theory. *Advances in Austrian Economics*, 20, 15–44. Retrieved from: http://doi.org/10.1108/S1529-213420160000020002

Cachanosky, N., & Lewin, P. (2016b, September). An empirical application of the EVA® framework to business cycles. *Review of Financial Economics*, 30, 60–67, http://doi.org/10.1016/j.rfe.2016.06.006

Cachanosky, N., & Lewin, P. (2018). The role of capital structure in Austrian business cycle theory. *Journal of Private Enterprise*, 8(2), 268–280.

Clark, J. B. (1893). The genesis of capital. *Yale Review*, 302–315.

Clark, J. B. (1988 [1888]). *Capital and Its Earnings*. New York, NY: Garland.

Cohen, A. J., & Harcourt, G. C. (2003). Whatever happened to the Cambridge Capital controversies? Journal of Econonomic Perspectives, 17(1), 199–214.

Dorfman, R. (1959a). A graphical exposition of Böhm-Bawerk's interest theory. *The Review of Economic Studies*, 26(2), 153–158.

Dorfman, R. (1959b). Waiting and the period of production. *The Quarterly Journal of Economics*, 73(3), 351–372.

Faber, M. (1979). *An Introduction to Modern Austrian Capital Theory.* New York, NY: Springer-Verlag.

Felipe, J., & Fisher, F. M. (2006). Aggregate production functions, neoclassical growth models and the aggregation problem. *Estudios de Economica Applicada*, 24(1), 127–163.

Felipe, J., & McCombie, J. S. (2014). The aggregate production function: 'not even wrong.' *Review of Political Economy*, 26(1), 60–84.

Fetter, F. A. (1977). *Capital, Interest and Rent: Essays in the Theory of Distribution.* Kansas City, MO: Sheed, Andrews and McMeel.

Fisher, F. M. (1993). *Aggregation: Aggregate Production Functions and Related Topics.* Cambridge, MA: MIT Press.

Fisher, F. M. (2005). Aggregate production functions: A pervasive but unpersuasive fairy tale. *Eastern Economic Journal*, 3, 489–491.

Fisher, I. (1906). *The Nature of Capital and Income.* London: Macmillan.

Fowler, R. F. (1934). *The Depreciation of Capital Analytically Considered.* London: P. S. King & Son.

Garrison, R. (2001). *Time and Money: The Macroeconomics of Capital Structure.* London: Routledge.

Garrison, R. W. (2006). Reflections on reswitching and roundaboutness. In R. Koppl, ed., *Money and Markets: Essays in Honor of Leland B. Yeager.* New York, NY: Routledge, 186–206

Hayek, F. A. (1931). *Prices and Production*, 2 edn. London: Routledge and Kegan Paul,1935.

Hayek, F. A. (1932). Capital consumption. In F. A. Hayek & R. Mcloughry, eds., *Money, Capital and Fluctuations, Early Essays, [1984].* (From *Welschaftliches Archiv* 36(1), 136–158, translated from the German "Kapitalaufzehrug" by Greta Heinz). Reprinted in *Capital and Interest* (Vol. 11 in *The Collected Works of F. A. Hayek*, L. H. White, ed.). Chicago: University of Chicago Press.

Hayek, F. A. (1934). On the relationship between investment and output. *Economic Journal*, 44(174), 207–231. As reprinted in F. A. Hayek (2015), chapter 6, 75–99.

Hayek, F. A. (1935). The maintenance of capital. *Economica, n.s.* 2(7), 241–276, as reprinted in F. A. Hayek (2015), chapter 10, 156–189.

Hayek, F. A. (1936a). The mythology of capital. *The Quarterly Journal of Economics*, 50(2), 199–228, as reprinted in F. A. Hayek (2015) chapter 8, 11–140.

Hayek, F. A. (1936b). Technical progress and excess capacity. Lecture delivered in April 1936, as reprinted in Hayek (2015), chapter 9, 141–155.

Hayek, F. A. (1937a). Economics and knowledge. Economica, n.s., IV, 33–54.

Hayek, F. A. (1937b). Investment that raises the demand for capital. *Review of Economics and Statistics*, 19(4), 174–177.

Hayek, F. A. (1939). *Profits, Interest and Investment and Other Essays on the Theory of Industrial Relations*. New York, NY: Augustus Kelly.

Hayek, F. A. (1941a). *The Pure Theory of Capital* (Vol. 12 of *The Collected Works of F. A. Hayek*, 2007, L. H. White, ed.) Chicago: University of Chicago Press.

Hayek, F. A. (1941b). Maintaining capital intact: Reply. *Economica, n.s.* 8(31), 276–288, as reprinted in Hayek (2015), chapter 12.

Hayek, F. A. (1994). *Hayek on Hayek, and Autobiographical Dialogue.* (S. K. L. Wenar, ed.). Chicago: University of Chicago Press. Republished by Liberty Fund, Indianapolis, 2008.

Hayek, F. A. (2015). *Capital and Interest* (Vol. 11 in *The Collected Works of F. A. Hayek*, L. H. White, Ed.) Chicago: University of Chicago Press.

Hicks, J. R. (1939). *Value and Capital*. Oxford: Oxford University Press.

Hicks, J. R. (1942). Maintaining capital intact: A further suggestion. *Economica n. s.*, 9(34), 174–179.

Hicks, J. R. (1973a). *Capital and Time: A Neo-Austrian Theory*. Oxford: Oxford University Press.

Hicks, J. R. (1973b). The Austrian theory of capital and its rebirth in modern economics. In J. R. Hicks, & W. Weber, Eds., *Carl Menger and the Austrian School of Economics*. Oxford: Clarendon Press. Reprinted in Hicks (1983), 96–102.

Hicks, J. R. (1976). Some questions of time in economics. In A. M. Tang & F. M. Westfield, eds., *Evolution, Welfare and Time in Economics*, Festschrift *in Honor of Nicholas Georgescu-Roegenr*. Lexington: Lexington Books. Reprinted in Hicks (1984), 263–280.

Hicks, J. R. (1979a). Is interest the price of a factor of production? In M. Rizzo, ed., *Time, Uncertainty and Disequilibrium*. Lexington: Lexington Books. Reprinted in Hicks (1983), 113–138.

Hicks, J. R. (1979b). *Causality in Economics*. Oxford: Basil Blackwell.

Hicks, J. R. (1983). *Classics and Moderns: Collected Essays on Economic Theory, Vol. III*. Cambridge: Harvard University Press.

Hicks, J. R. (1984). *The Economics of John Hicks*. Selected and with an introduction by Dieter Helm. Oxford: Basil Blackwell.

Hodgson, G. M. (2014). What is capital? Economists and sociologists have changed its meaning: Should it be changed back? *Cambridge Journal of Economics*, 38, 1063–1086.

Horwitz, S. (2011). Contrasting concepts of capital: Yet another look at the Hayek-Keynes debate. *The Journal of Private Enterprise*, 27(1), 9–27.

Jevons, W. S. (1888 [1871]). *The Theory of Political Economy*. London: Macmillan & Co. Retrieved from: www.econlib.org/library/YPDBooks/Jevons/jvnPE.html

Keynes, J. M. (1936). *The General Theory of Employment, Interest and Money*. London: Macmillan.

Kirzner, I. M. (1966). *An Essay on Capital*. New York, NY: Augustus M. Kelly.

Koppl, R. (2014). *From Crisis to Confidence: Macroeconomics after the Crash*. London: Institute of Economic Affairs.

Lachmann, L. M. (1947). Complementarity and substitution in the theory of capital. *Economica*, 14, 108–119.

Lachmann, L. M. (1948). Investment repercussions. *The Quarterly Journal of Economics*, 62(5), 698–713. Reprinted in Lachmann (1994), chapter 9.

Lachmann, L. M. (1956). *Capital and Its Structure*. Mission, KS: Sheed, Andrews and McMeel, 2nd edn 1978.

Lachmann, L. M. (1986). *The Market as Economic Process*. Oxford: Basil Blackwell.

Lachmann, L. M. (1994). *Expectations and the Meaning of Institutions: Essays in Economics by Ludwig M. Lachmann* (D. Lavoie, ed.). New York, NY: Routledge.

Lester, R. B., & Wolf, J. S. (2013). The empirical relevance of the Mises–Hayek theory of the trade cycle. *Review of Austrian Economics*, 26(4), 433–461.

Lewin, P. (1997). Capital and time: Variations on a Hicksian theme. *Advances in Austrian Economics*, 4, 63–74.

Lewin, P. (1998). The firm, money, and economic calculation: Considering the institutional nexus of market production. *American Journal of Economics and Sociology*, 57(4), 499–512.

Lewin, P. (2011 [1999]). *Capital in Disequilibrium*. Auburn, AL: Ludwig von Mises Institute.

Lewin, P. (2013). Hayek and Lachmann and the complexity of capital. In R. Garrison, ed., *The Elgar Companion to Hayek*. Cheltenham: Edward Elgar, chapter 8.

Lewin, P., & Cachanosky, N. (2016). A financial framework for understanding macroeconomic cycles. *Journal of Private Enterprise*, 33(2), 21–32.

Lewin, P., & Cachanosky, N. (2018a). Value and capital: Austrian capital theory, retrospect and prospect. *Review of Austrian Economics*, 3(1), 1–26.

Lewin, P., & Cachanosky, N. (2018b). The average period of production: The history of an idea. *Journal of the History of Economic Thought*, 40(1), 81–98.

Lewin, P., & Cachanosky, N. (2018c). Substance and semantics: The question of capital. *Journal of Economic Behavior & Organization*, 150(June), 423–431.

Luther, W. J., & Cohen, M. (2014). An empirical analysis of the Austrian business cycle theory. *Atlantic Economic Journal*, 42(2), 153–169. Retrieved from: http://doi.org/10.1007/s11293-014-9415-5

Macaulay, F. R. (1938). *The Movements of Interest Rates. Bond Yields and Stock Prices in the United States since 1856*. New York, NY: National Bureau of Economic Research.

McClure, J. E., Spectre, L. C., & Chandler, D. (2018). Hayek's tacit knowledge. *SSRN*. Retrieved from: https://papers.ssrn.com/sol3/papers.cfm?abstract_id=3213973

Menger, C. (1871 [translated 1976]). *Principles of Economics*. (J. D. Hoselitz, trans.) Auburn, AL: Ludwig von Mises Institute, republished 2007.

Menger, C. (1888). Zur Theorie des Kapitals. *Jahrbücher für Nationalökonomie und Statistik*, 17, 1–49.

Menger, C. (1892). On the origin of money. *The Economic Journal*, 2(6), 239–255.

Mises, L. v. (1912). *The Theory of Money and Credit*. (H. Batson, trans.). Indianapolis, IN: Liberty Fund, 1981.

Mises, L. v. (1920). Economic calculation in the socialist commonwealth. In F. A. Hayek, ed., *Collectivist Economic Planning*. London: Routledge and Sons, 87–103.

Mises, L. v. (1922 [2011]). *Socialism: An Economic and Sociological Analysis*. Indianapolis, IN: Liberty Fund.Mises, L. v. (1949, 4th edn [1996]). *Human Action*. Irvington on Hudson, NY: Foundation for Economic Education.

Mises, L. v. [1931](2003). Inconvertible capital. In L. V. Mises, *Epistemological Problems of Economics*, 3rd edn (G. C. Reisman, trans.). Auburn, AL: Mises Institute, 231–246. Retrieved from: https://mises.org/library/epistemological-problems-economics

Mises, L. v. (2003 [1933], 3rd edn). *Epistemological Problems of Economics*. (G. B. Reisman, trans.) Auburn, AL: Ludwig von Mises Institute. Retrieved from: https://mises.org/library/epistemological-problems-economics

Mulligan, R. F. (2002). A Hayekian analysis of the structure of production. *Quarterly Journal of Austrian Economics*, 5(2), 17–33.

Murphy, R. P. (2015). *Choice, Cooperation, Enterprise and Human Action*. Oakland, CA: Independent Institute.

Osborne, M. (2005). On the computation of a formula for the duration of a bond that yields precise results. *Quarterly Review of Economics and Finance*, 45(1), 161–183.

Osborne, M. (2014). *Multiple Interest Rate Analysis: Theory and Applications*. Basingstoke, UK: Palgrave.

Pigou, A. C. (1935). Net income and capital depletion. *Economic Journal*, 45(178), 235–241.

Pigou, A. C. (1941). Maintaining capital intact. *Economica, n. s.* 8(31), 271–273, as reprinted in Hayek (2015), chapter 11.

Pigou, A. C. (1946 [1932]). *The Economics of Welfare*, 4th edn. London: Macmillan & Co.

Piketty, T. (2014). *Capital in the Twenty First Century*. Cambridge, MA: Harvard University Press.

Powell, B. (2002). Explaining Japan's recession. *Quarterly Journal of Austrian Economics*, 5(2), 35–50.

Rothbard, M. (2009 [1962]). *Man, Economy and State with Power of the Market (the Scholar's edition)*. Auburn, AL: Ludwig von Mises Institute.

Samuelson, P. A. (1966). A summing up. *Quarterly Journal of Economics*, 80(4), 568–583.

Schumpeter, J. (1942 [2010]). *Capitalism, Socialism and Democracy*. London: George Allen and Unwin.

Schumpeter, J. (1954). *History of Economics Analysis*. New York, NY: Oxford University Press.

Scott, M. (1984). Maintaining capital intact. *Oxford Economic Papers, n. s. Supplement: Economic Theory and Hicksian Themes*, 36, 59–78.

Smith, A. (2002 [1776]). *An Inquiry into the Nature and Causes of the Wealth of Nations*. Retrieved from: www.amazon.com/gp/product/B000JQUA6E/ref=pd_lpo_k2_dp_sr_3?pf_rd_p=486539851&pf_rd_s=lpo-top-stripe-1&pf_rd_t=201&pf_rd_i=0879757051&pf_rd_m=ATVPDKIKX0DER&pf_rd_r=02S2KGTFTW2BPYBN84EG

Solow, R. (1956). A contribution to the theory of economic growth. *The Quarterly Journal of Economics*, 70(1), 65–94.

Swan, T. (1956). Economic growth and capital accumulation. *Economic Record*, 32(2), 334–361.

Uhr, C. (1960). *Economic Doctrines of Knut Wisksell*. Berkeley: University of California Press.

White, L. H. (2007). Introduction to Hayek (1941).

Wicksell, K. (1934 [1911]). *Lectures on Political Economy,* Vol. 1. London: Routledge.

Yeager, L. B. (1976). Toward understanding some paradoxes in capital theory. *Economic Inquiry*, 14(3).

Young, A. T. (2005). Reallocating labor to initiate changes in capital structure: Hayek revisited. *Economic Letters*, 3, 275–282.

Young, A. T. (2012). The time structure of production in the US, 2002–2009. *Review of Austrian Economics*, 25(2), 77–92. Retrieved from: http://doi.org/10.1007/s11138-011–0158–0

Acknowledgments

We received very helpful feedback, both substantive and editorial, on earlier drafts from Steve Horwitz, Bill Tulloh, and Roger Garrison. We owe Roger Koppl a debt of gratitude for first suggesting to us we further explore the concept of bond duration in relation to the average period of production. Whatever shortcomings remain are our sole responsibility.

Cambridge Elements ☰

Austrian Economics

Peter Boettke
George Mason University

Peter Boettke is a Professor of Economics and Philosophy at George Mason University, the BB&T Professor for the Study of Capitalism, and the director of the F. A. Hayek Program for Advanced Study in Philosophy, Politics, and Economics at the Mercatus Center at George Mason University.

About the Series

This series is primarily focused on contemporary developments in the Austrian School of Economics and its relevance to the methodological and analytical debates at the frontier of social science and humanities research, and the continuing relevance of the Austrian School of Economics for the practical affairs of public policy throughout the world.

Cambridge Elements $\equiv$

Austrian Economics

Elements in the Series

The Decline and Rise of Institutions: A Modern Survey of the Austrian Contribution to the Economic Analysis of Institutions
Liya Palagashvili, Ennio Piano, and David Skarbek

Austrian Capital Theory: A Modern Survey of the Essentials
Peter Lewin and Nicolas Cachanosky

A full series listing is available at: www.cambridge.org/EAEC

Printed in the United States
By Bookmasters